BEST SCOTCH OR ORDINARY?

A North East Publican's Tale

BILL KELL

Published by:
Woodhorn Press
c/o Honeysuckle Cottage
Widdrington
Morpeth
Northumberland

© Copyright Bill Kell, 1996

ISBN 0 9523422 4 3

ACKNOWLEDGEMENTS
The author wishes to thank Mike Kirkup for transforming his manuscript into its present form; to Jack Wallace who was always around the *Portland* taking photographs; and to Jim Merrington of Newcastle Breweries for his help and support.

Front cover design by *Ralph Liddell*
Printed by *Martins the Printers Ltd, Berwick on Tweed*
Typeset by *Ed Skelly*

BEST SCOTCH OR ORDINARY?

To Jake.

Best Wishes
For Xmas '96

Bill Kell

CONTENTS

	Page
Young Kell, the Apprentice, 1942	5
Old Kell, the Showman	17
Kell Jnr goes to the Dogs, 1947	23
The *Portland*'s post-war Characters	32
Learning the Bar Trade...	
at Hexham	46
at Winlaton	50
at Crook	52
Kell takes a Bride...	
...and the *Crown and Anchor*, Low Walker	54
Jackie Milburn lends a hand	59
The *Traveller's Rest*, Blyth	88
Back to the *Portland*, 1955	96
Ashington's Swinging Sixties	116
The Kells *Up The Junction*	135
Last Orders, Please	145

YOUNG KELL, THE APPRENTICE, 1942

The *Portland Hotel* in Ashington was built around 1890. It was a private concern, commissioned and purchased by a Mr Forbes. By all accounts it was something special for its day, set in its own land to the side while, at the rear, were stables, a coach-house, pig sties and even its own abattoir. Upstairs maids serviced the guests' bedrooms which also provided accommodation for the owner's family.

Mr Forbes bottled his own beer. A horse and cart picked up barrels of *Guinness* and *Bass* from Ashington Railway Station and transported them along Station Road to the hotel. An empty bottle with the label 'Forbes Best Bitter' was later discovered in the graveyard of the Holy Sepulchre, the parish church.

Right next door to the hotel was the *Coronation Bar*, run by old Bill Tiplady, a strapping six-footer doubling as a bouncer who later managed the *Plough Inn* at Ellington. The *Coronation Bar* – named in 1901 when Edward VII was crowned – was mainly used by the local miners, especially on a pay-day Friday when money needed to be changed by the leaders of each set of hewers and then distributed to the individual colliers. Further along were greenhouses, also belonging to the *Portland*, and a fine orchard with apple trees, destined to become Institute Road many years later.

Sylvester Strong, a co-operative drapery worker, was the next owner, having married Mr Forbes's daughter. He was hard hit by the miners' strike of 1921, but it was the General Strike of 1926 which signalled the end for the over-generous Sylvester who never recovered the credit he gave out to the Ashington miners during the long drawn out stoppage.

Enter big Bill Sanderson, the Morpeth 'pop' man with the ten-gallon hat. Sanderson bought the *Portland* and also the *Widdrington Inn*, *Lynemouth Hotel*, and the *Queen's Head* in Morpeth. In 1937, *McEwan's* the brewers came to Sanderson looking to buy the *Queen's Head*. The astute Morpeth gadgie said they could have it on condition they took a package of pubs which included the *Portland*.

The bargain was struck and it is believed that the going price for the *Portland* was in the region of £12,000.

In 1938, *McEwan's* brought in my dad, Bill Kell snr, to manage the *Portland* for them, leaving Sanderson grumbling: "If I'd known Kell was going to be manager I wouldn't have let it go!"

My father had five part-time barmen, all miners, under head barman, Kit Stoddart, an ex-pitman himself who was eventually called back to work at the Colliery when mining became a reserved occupation during the second world war.

The *Portland* was a busy pub, one of only three in the town, the others being the *Grand Hotel* and *North Seaton Hotel*, always referred to as the *White Elephant*. But there were twenty-two workingmen's clubs, all in the space of a few hundred yards, in direct competition, so our beer had to be tip top and the service good and fast. My father was always smartly dressed with black jacket and pinstripe trousers. The barmen all had to wear clean white aprons with shirt sleeves rolled up. Old Kell was a top-class publican who could converse with anyone, sing a song or tell a joke – as the saying goes: he kept a 'good house'.

Prior to coming to the *Portland*, father had been managing the *Gloucester Inn* in Gateshead's High West Street. He was then getting £2 per week, but was offered the *Portland* for £2.10s, with free accommodation. He was to tell me later that it was not the extra ten bob that was the inducement – he wanted me and my sister Dora out of that environment; he also fancied the challenge of a new pub in a relatively new town.

Bill Norrie was the outside manager and he held the licence and took stock once a month. My father, as manager, was in charge of the day-to-day running of the pub. The wages bill had to be kept below ten per cent, never higher or there would be an enquiry. Full-time barmen received thirty bob a week; part-timers got two-and-a-tanner a night, same as the weekend waiter who worked from 7 pm till 10 pm. The lady piano player was paid five shillings for each of the two nights she performed. One of the part-time barmen was Billy Smith who went into the Royal Air Force and was later a steward of the *Middle Market* or 'Kickin' Cuddy' as it was called. Another was Jimmy Locke who I believe is still collecting glasses in the bar-lounge at the *Comrades*.

Young Kell, the Apprentice, 1942

During the second world war, as father was too old for active service, he was directed to work as a full-time officer in the Civil Defence Rescue Service, doing twelve-hour shifts, manning the local ARP headquarters. This left mum to run the pub for the other twelve hours of the day. And so it was that, in 1942, I was conscripted into the position of apprentice barman. But that wasn't my first job.

Having been brought up in a pub, I had a vague idea about what was required of me, but, on account of me having asthma, my parents were advised to get me a fresh-air job. So they bought a share in a coal delivery business owned by Bobby Cook who had stables behind the *Portland*. I was to be a coalman!

The business consisted of three horses with carts; one flat lorry and two cowp carts. I was thin and scrawny then and just putting the harness on my seventeen-hands cross Clydesdale was a nightmare. I had to climb on top of the manger simply to put this huge collar over its head.

My job was to deliver coal to local business establishments and private houses: four tons in the morning and five tons in the afternoon. It was all shovelled on and off the lorry, or on to the cowp cart, tipped at the door, then shovelled into the customer's coalhouse.

Duke Street Coal Depot opened at eight in the morning and I was usually there waiting for the gates to open. Most days there were lads standing at the gate, willing to help you load and unload. They were unemployable 'daft' lads who worked hard for the sixpence they were given for hoying the coal into the cree. But if it started to rain, or it was hard shovelling off the top of a railway wagon, these so-called 'daft' lads would go home and leave you to get on with it. Not so daft, eh.

Two ex-miners worked at the Depot in those days, one was Tommy Rump and the other had a glass eye. The pair were kind men who helped me to load the coal. It was hard, back-breaking work, with wintertime, because it was so busy, being the worst. Summers were comparatively cushy.

One day I had to take a load of horse manure (another lousy job) across to Kit Latimer's place at New Moor – a distance of about two miles. On arriving, I had to back the horse down a narrow path between the gardens. Except that I couldn't budge the horse: it refused to be backed-up.

Mrs Latimer came to my rescue: "Aa'll give ye a hand, son. Aa've worked on farms wiv horses aall me life."

She grasped the bridle and backed the horse a hundred yards to where the muck had to be tipped; took the pin out of the cowp cart and tipped the load like a true professional – what a woman!

One weekend, Ossie Rogers, a local horse dealer, called at the pub. After a few drinks with my dad, he said: "Aye, Kell, Aa hear young Bill's gone into the coal trade."

"He has that, Oz, and he's mekin a canny job on't."

"Ye wouldn't be lookin' for a fresh horse by any chance?" asked Ossie.

"Funny ye should say that, Oz, cos we do need a replacement. The one wiv got is just aboot knackered, as they say."

"Then look no further, Billy boy. Aa just happen to have the smartest animal around these parts, and it's gannin cheap. Eighty quid. But it'll repay ye wiv interest in six months."

Now eighty quid was a lot of money then, but father was a bit desperate, so the pair of them gave the customary slap of the hands and the deal was struck.

The horse was delivered on the Sunday morning. But little Bobby Cook took one look at the nag and shook his head, saying "Aa'm hevin nowt to dee with that flamin' thing."

"Hoo's that, Bobby?" asked my father, a little taken aback.

"Whey, man, can ye not see? It's a bloody circus horse! No good whatsoever for cartin' coal."

The white horse stood seventeen hands with skinny legs. Indeed, as it turned out, it *had* performed tricks in a circus which had folded when war broke out. As Bobby had refused point blank to take the horse out, muggins got the job.

As we placed the harness over the horse's head on that first Monday morning, the nag, which we had unimaginatively named Snowy, was shivering with fear. We eventually got him into the limmers attached to the flat cart. Bobby said: "Ye'd better get one o' the lads to hold him till he gets used to the work."

Off we went, Snowy prancing and dancing like a ballerina, down to the coal depot. I drove straight on to the weighbridge so that Jimmy Little, the manager, could weigh us. By then Snowy was in an extremely skitterish state, sliding about on the slippery metal weighbridge like a four-legged Christopher Dean.

The lad with me held the horse's head while I went into the

pokey little office. Jimmy Little said: "Whaat Cheor, Bill. What hev ye got there thi day? Bit flighty, isn't it? Whaat sort o' coal do ye want this mornin'?"

"A load of Trebles, please, Ji ... er ... Mr Little."

You had to show respect to that man.

"Ye'll hev to fill off the top of the wagon, Aa'm afraid, Bill. We canna drop the doors on a wagon of Trebles, ye knaa."

I knew that only too well. "OK," I said, and off we trotted up the yard to the wagon holding the Bothal House Trebles. I told my helper to hold the horse while I climbed into the wagon which was almost empty, making it impossible for me to see over the top.

As the first shovelful of coal clattered into the cart, Snowy reared up like a frightened jack-rabbit and galloped off at full pelt down the depot yard to the timberyard, next door. The first I knew of this was when I peeked my head over the top of the railway wagon and saw the horse and cart disappearing through piles and piles of pit props.

The cart was a complete write-off, looking as though Damon Hill had run into the back of it. We eventually caught up with the horse: 'Poor Snowy. Aah.' There it was, quivering with fright, cut and bruised, and standing with limmers still attached. We got him back to the stables, washed down and patched up.

Dad soon had a phone call from an irate timberyard manager: "Hey, Kell, do ye knaa hoo much damage yor lad and that crazy horse has done doon here? It's ganna cost ye an arm and a leg, Kell, for this one. Aa'm just warnin' ye!"

Dad tried to talk Ossie into taking Snowy back. No dice. He refused categorically: "A deal's a deal, Bill. Sorry. But Aa want me money."

Bill Kell senior realised that he had made a bloomer and began to wrack his brain for a way out.

We had a regular customer then called Alfie Gooch: a travelling showman whose menagerie had been stranded in People's Park when the war broke out. All travelling had been suspended. He lived in the corner of the Park in a caravan with his wife and three children: Sadie, Lonzo and young Tommy. Mrs Gooch was the show's tatooed lady. Alfie often did odd jobs here and there to make ends meet.

About a couple of weeks after the 'Snowy debacle', dad approached Alfie with a proposition: "Hoo would ye like to mek thorty bob, Alfie?"

"What do I have to do, Mr Kell?" asked the cagey showman.

"Do ye knaa where Ellington is?"

Alfie nodded.

"Whey, Aa've got a horse that Aa want ye to tek doon there and put into a field, belaangin' to a ... to a friend o' mine."

"OK, Mr Kell. I will take the horse down straight away."

"Oh, no, no, Alfie. Just howld on a minute. Aa want it took doon when it's dark. At two o'clock in the mornin', to be precise," said father with a confidential twist of his head and the wink of an eye.

"Oh, I see," said Alfie with a sly rub of his nose. "I will see to that for you, Mr Kell, and no further questions asked."

Snowy was duly returned to its original owner, and we heard no more of the matter.

Lonzo Gooch was a real character, about my own age. He had been sent to my school at St Aidan's and put into the same class where I had the job of teaching him to read. Lonzo was extremely interested in keeping chickens. Every day he brought in newspaper cuttings for me to read to him. And they always had photos of poultry in them. He also kept bringing in the same advert: *Karswood Spice, for Laying Hens.*

Lonzo and I liked going to Ashington swimming baths. Just after the humiliation of Dunkirk, the British Tommy was ordered to learn how to swim because of heavy losses through drowning. So troops who were based in the Ashington area used the baths almost every day.

The soldiers swam two-lengths of the baths in full kit. Lonzo and I watched their antics with glee, especially when one or more of them sank like stones after only one length. That was the signal for a sergeant physical training instructor (PTI) to dive in and haul them to the surface.

One day a squaddie went under; his steel helmet came off and sank quickly to the bottom of the pool. Lonzo dived in, brought the helmet out, stuck it on his head, and began marching up and down the side of the pool, giving everyone the Nazi Heil Hitler salute. He then dived in with the helmet still attached to his head, sank like a ton of bricks and didn't come up. The weight of the steel helmet kept his head firmly on the bottom, his legs thrashing about like an upside-down bumblebee. He almost drowned. Fortunately, the PTI dived in and pulled him out. Lonzo didn't do any more tricks that day.

One cold, dark winter's morning, I was headed up Ashington's main street to the coal depot. I sat hunched up on the lorry, feeling miserable, trying to keep warm. On the other side of Station Road were three miners on their bikes, heading for the colliery. One of them waved at me and shouted: "Whaat Cheor, Bobby," and pedalled on.
 Bobby? Who the ...? And then the penny dropped: they thought I was Bobby Cook. Bobby Cook, a small, round-shouldered man with a chesty cough! It was then I knew that the coal trade was not for me. That very night I told my dad that I wanted to pack in the coal business and start full-time as a barman at the *Portland*.
 Dad didn't give me any argument. "Ye can start the morn, son."

My job as trainee barman consisted of doing all the dirty jobs: scrubbing the cellar floor; sorting the empty bottles; stocking the shelves with wiped and polished new beer bottles; scrubbing the glass drainers until they sparkled; cleaning the beer, wine and spirit glasses till they shone; cleaning the filter bags and the urinals and the spitoons and the ... Then it was time to open the pub: 11 am.
 Dad was an outstanding salesman. To prove the point ... one of my jobs was to fill wine bottles. We had a regular quota of British wine which we sold for three shillings and sixpence a bottle. I washed out and filled the bottles, knocked in a cork with a wooden mallet, put on a silver seal and then stuck on a *British Ruby Wine* label.
 The casks of wine we used came in three different sizes: nine, fourteen and twenty-eight gallons. I mentioned to dad that there was a build-up of wine in the cellars.
 "Hoo much hev we got?" he asked.
 "'Boot forty gallons, altogether."
 "Aa'll tell ye what we'll do, Bill. Clean off aall o' those Ruby Wine labels and just leave the silver seal on top o' the bottles."
 He then made out a printed notice which read: **'Vintage Port. Two pounds ten shillings a bottle. Limited supply only.'** We sold the lot in a month!

Kit Stoddart had the job of filling the whisky which arrived every month in a six-gallon Grey Hen which was a large stone jar covered with basket weave and sealed with wax. The whisky bottling was done on Tuesdays. This was the signal for Kit to stagger out of the cellar, mortal drunk, saying in a slurred voice, false teeth wobbling all over his mouth: "Aa'll hev to gan hyem, boss. Them whisky fumes hev affected is again." It was then I had to volunteer to see him across the road to his house in the Eleventh Row.

On his day off, Kit always dressed in his best black suit, black top hat, white silk scarf and bowler hat. Then he would proceed to visit every pub and club in Ashington, starting at the *White Elephant* and working his way through the town. He didn't always make it! One night he landed at the *Portland* at nine o'clock, drunk as a lord. He went behind the bar and switched off all the beer taps, shouting: "Ishtime, Ladiesh 'nd Shentlemen, Pleashe."

Old Kell was standing in his usual place at the top end of the bar when this was taking place. He turned to me and said: "What the hell's the matter wiv him noo?"

We got Bob Hart to take him home.

One night during the war we got three strangers in from Newcastle: two busty blondes and a fella you could have called a *Spiv*. He wore a brown pin-striped suit with a frock coat and a brown Homberg. The two 'ladies' wore cheap short-length fur coats. Right Toonies. One of the women had come to see her father who lived in a flat above a shop in Station Road.

In those days, certain drinks were in short supply so we never had a great variety from which to choose. But during the course of the evening that trio supped a lotta stuff. Getting on towards closing time, the two women fell out over who should 'have' the *Spiv*. They began to swear and fight, throwing punches at each other like two prizefighters. One fell on top of the other, tearing out her hair together with lumps of cheap fur coat, blinding and cursing all the while.

We eventually managed to get them out through the side door. During the melee their mutual friend had legged it out of the pub. We never saw any of them again, but we were sweeping fur off the floor for weeks afterwards.

A fully operational RAF station was situated at Acklington, eight miles away. At one time, Princess Margaret's beau, Peter Townsend was there, only a squadron leader then. Occasionally we got the Brylcreem boys down for a night out.

Townsend and some of his young aircrew came in one night to celebrate a mate's birthday. They began drinking *McEwan's Special Beer*, our strongest draught ale. They became boisterous and began emulating the *Student Prince* by flinging glasses on to the floor after they had emptied them. They were made of thick wartime glass with stout handles which took a lot of breaking. However, one of them hit a radiator pipe and smashed into tiny pieces.

My father tried to calm things down: "Aa'll right, lads, settle doon noo. Hoo's in charge of yous lot, anyway?"

Townsend stepped forward: "Well, I suppose I am, actually."

Old Kell squared his shoulders to the dare-devil pilot: "Hey, lad, them glasses is like gold to get a'haad of. Do ye not knaa that there's a bloody war on?"

It was the time of the *Bevin Boys*, young lads who had come to Ashington from all over the country to work in the mines. About two hundred of them lived in a Miners' Hostel which stood behind the Wesleyan Central Hall on Woodhorn Road. The majority were Scotsmen with egos as big as Ben Nevis.

I was then in charge of my own bar at the *Portland*, called the Buffet. Behind the bar I kept a pre-war *Cossar* radiogram which was there for my own personal enjoyment as well as the customers'.

The BBs were all good dancers, much admired by the local 'talent'. One Scots lad who was a regular came in one night and enquired: "Ha'e ye no Jimmy Shand records, pal?"

"Sorry, mate, but Aa've nivvor even heard o' Jimmy Shand."

Scotty couldn't believe his ears.

"Och, away! Ye mean to tell me that ye've no heard o' the great Jimmy Shand what plays the Scottish reels?"

"No."

"If Aa bring some o' ma own records in, will ye play 'em for us, pal?"

"Anything to oblige," I said.

On the Friday night Jock came in with some old 78s. I put them on the wobbly turntable, and everyone thoroughly enjoyed the music – including the Ashingtonians. As the evening wore on, the Scots began to take to the floor, one at a time to start with, but by half past nine they were all up doing reels, jigs and God-knows-what. A Scot named Brice O'Brien stood up on a table and showed everyone what a good dancer he was.

Father walked into the Buffet. Dancing in there was unheard of, but dancing on the table was something else. Dad beckoned for Brice to get down. He took out a pocket-book and pen, saying: "'nd what might yor name be, laddie?"

"McDonald, sor."

Father wrote the name in his book: 'McDONALD'. "'nd yor forst name?"

"Ramsey, sor."

Father began writing and spelling: 'RAMS...'. He suddenly pulled up short, realising the Scot was having a joke at his expense. He looked across at me, scowled, snapped shut his little book, shook his head, and walked out.

One of the Scots BBs called Williams was as black as coal itself. Every weekend he came into the Buffet and proceeded to get charmingly drunk. "I'm not like this lot y'know, Bill," he would say in a refined accent, gesturing towards the rowdies in the corner. "I'm from Edinburgh."

The Christmas holidays came around and most of the BBs went home to enjoy the festive season. The few who stayed behind that year decided to have a proper Christmas dinner in the Hostel. A large turkey was bought, cooked on Christmas Eve, and left overnight in the canteen kitchen. On Christmas morning the turkey had gone AWOL. Not a sign of it anywhere. They hunted high and low, eventually going into the dormitory where Williams lay snoring like a pig. And there, nestling under his bed, was a pile of turkey bones, all that remained of their Christmas dinner.

Friday night at the *Portland* was quiet, but Saturday was always busy. The rest of the week we had our regulars to keep us ticking over. There was no television, so the pub was the focal point of entertainment, providing stimulating conversation and a place to meet. We had a wireless in the bar where we could listen to the news, racing and boxing. The Big Fight was always a good night in

Managed by dad in 1937. I am little lad 2nd left, Dad is front centre wearing mac and plus-fours. Mother is kneeling in dress. Sister Dora and two cousins Betty and Michael are also in front row.

My mother Annie was a bonny lass in 1924.

Ye Owld Bill Kell managed *Ye Olde Plough Inn*, Bigg Market, Newcastle, in 1926.

My favourite car was an MG, bought from Gibson's Garage in 1949.

Butlins, Pwllheli, 1947. Back row: George Nichol, Jack Tweddle, Winston Ball, Alec Cummings, Dougie Scott. Front: Les Stevenson, Bill Kell, and Roy Stewart of Linton.

Butlins, Ayr, 1949. Rusty and I clowning around with Buck Milburn, Bobby Langdown and their wives.

Rusty puts Kell into the stocks.

The Kells took good care of the FA Cup when Jackie Milburn brought it to the *Portland* in 1951.

The *Crown and Anchor* lads wore Milburn's international caps with pride in 1951.

Me and the *Crown and Anchor* 'look-out' man, blind Alfie Miekle. Note Milburn memorabilia on left.

Dad serves cowboy Fred Curry and his horse on the *Portland* steps in 1953. Looking on are Bob Hart, Matty Morris, Eddie Hall, Jackie Robson, Bill Bell, Vic Ford, Jimmy Rogers and *'Oosh-ye-bugger'* Jimmy Hindmarsh in trilby hat.

1956 RAFA Carnival Baby Show spoof with Kell and Alec Cummings taking 1st prize at Portland Park.

Sally Gladson was a regular in the back bar of the *Portland*, a staunch socialist who always drank a gill of bitter between dragging on her clay pipe.

Maple Street newspaper vendor, Charlie 'Peace' Richardson, was another *Portland* character.

The *Portland's* own Sixties pop-group: Bill Kell, Bill Oliver, Sid Jackson, Hoss on vocals, Joe Kelly on drums, plus two others.

Eric Nichol did a great impression of Al Jolson. That's Ray Poxton sitting, left, and Hollings on drums.

the bar. They would all come in and get settled in to listen to such fighters as Randy Turpin, Bruce Woodcock, Sugar Ray Robinson and many others: all favourites with the customers.

When the war ended there were still shortages of everything. The lads were coming home, being demobbed with their utility suits and trilby hats and small cardboard boxes. They all had plenty of money; demob money they called it, and a lot of that was spent in the pubs and clubs. One of the lads was called Buck Milburn, an exceptional accordion player. Whenever he came into the Bar my dad encouraged him to play a small accordion that I had, and everyone would join in the fun. We had a part-time barman called Fred Curry who could dance like Fred Astaire. We cleared the long counter in the bar of glasses and he tap danced up and down the counter; as a finale he would jump off the counter and do the splits on the bar floor. They would all take turns at singing a song and whatever the quality of the performance they were always applauded afterwards; it was all good fun.

My father realised Buck's potential and asked if he would like to work weekends playing the accordion for him in the Portland Music Room. Buck was rather reluctant because he said his instrument wasn't up to scratch and he was saving to get an amplified accordion that was new on the market, but they cost £200. My father arranged to buy him the accordion on condition that Buck played for him until it was paid off. Buck accepted on condition that we also employed a drummer friend of his, Jimmy Bacon, who called himself 'Max Bacon' after a well known drummer of the time.

They played to full houses for months and years. During this time Buck and I became good friends and he would always approach me first with any new ideas he had about the band – so I could smooth the way with my father – especially if it was going to cost money. At that time there was a popular tune recorded by Ethel Smith on the new electric organ called *Tico Tico*, she played it at a very fast Samba time! This intrigued Buck and he played it on the accordion, but he would have loved to have tried it on the electric organ which was unobtainable in England at that time.

One Saturday morning Buck came into *The Portland* just after 11 am opening time. He was very excited. "Bill, I've just seen a Harmonium in Louis Johnson's sale rooms. It's got a very fast keyboard and we could amplify it with a contact microphone through the speakers and call it an electric organ. We can go and bid for it this afternoon; it shouldn't cost much."

So we went up to the sale rooms and bid for the Harmonium. It was old but in perfect condition, and we got it for £3-10-0. We brought it back to the *Portland* on the drop-down boot of my father's old pre-war Morris 14 HP car. We had nothing to tie it on with, so Buck walked behind the car holding the Harmonium, and I drove in first gear from the sale rooms to the *Portland*.

We spent the next few days fixing the organ with contact mikes and we had fluorescent strip lighting in every position: top, back and sides of the organ. There was only one snag; you had to pedal the organ to play it. To get around this we fitted a half circular curtain rail around the front of the organ so you couldn't see Buck's legs peddling like hell. It was billed as *'Buck Milburn on the Electric Organ'*. They came from miles around to see this new organ; my father had to put Bob Hart on the door of the Music Room to regulate the flow of visitors – so many out, so many in.

'Tico Tico' was flogged to death every night Buck played. Occasionally Buck would get a painful cramp in the legs through peddling the organ, and he would have to have massage from his father, Old Buck. But the show had to go on. This was showbusiness, and my father encouraged us as long as it didn't cost too much money.

Old Kell, the Showman

Father was a showman and he had served his time with an international showman. His name was Tommy Burns, Heavyweight Champion of the World. On his retirement from the Ring he had taken over the *Forth Hotel* in Pink Lane, Newcastle, opposite the Central Station. This would be about 1921. My mother, Annie, worked for Tommy Burns as buffet barmaid, upstairs on the first floor. She was then twenty years old and a very beautiful woman, with an attractive personality. This was the criteria for a job as buffet barmaid in the centre of the City of Newcastle in the 1920s.

Mother told me that Tommy Burns was a caring and a very gentle man, a good business man and, being an ex-world champion, a popular man with all the local sporting fraternity. He was also a devout Catholic convert.

One incident happened on the morning of St Patrick's Day. Tommy had arranged to have bowls of shamrock placed on the counters of the bars with packets of pins beside them, so that his Catholic customers could avail themselves of a small bunch to pin in their lapels. One of my mother's morning regulars was a large red-faced uncouth, know-all of a man, who made a living buying and selling things. It was his habit every time he came in to clap his hands together and say 'good morning, Annie' and then hang his bowler hat on one of the beer pump handles.

Mother didn't like this, or him! This particular day he was the first customer to come in. He noticed the bowls of shamrock, and walked up to the bar where the cruet stand sat; he took out the salt cellar and proceeded to salt the shamrock and eat it. He ate the whole bowl of shamrock. My mother called down stairs and told Tommy Burns what had happened. This was sacrilege in Tommy's eyes; he rushed into the Buffet and took hold of the man who hadn't a clue what was happening. The former world heavyweight threw him downstairs then turned and took the bowler hat off the beer pump handle and threw that after him.

Tommy boxed an exhibition match at St James' Hall, Newcastle, in 1921 and put on a show at the Hippodrome Theatre in 1926. Soon after he went back home to Canada. During this time my father and mother had married. Father took a small pub in the Bigg Market called *Ye Olde Plough*. He took the pub in partnership with George Peety who had a tailor's shop above the pub. The Bigg Market was a bustling place in those days, with rows of market stalls from Grainger Street corner down to the Town Hall. Father got most of the stall holders in the pub. On weekends they came from all over the country, selling everything. One man from Glasgow asked if dad could take delivery of some goods for him as he had used the name of the pub for the order. Dad agreed, and a large box arrived a few days later. It was full of tiny wooden salve boxes with wooden lids, about the size of a ten-pence piece across and half an inch deep. The Scotman asked if he could use the cellar to mix some salve to fill the boxes for the weekend market. As he was a good customer, dad allowed him the use of the pub cellar to mix the stuff. The Scotsman brought with him a large bowl, an ordinary kitchen knife, about two stone of white lard and a big bottle of green ink. He mixed the lard and green ink in the bowl and filled the small wooden salve boxes with the knife, then popped on the lids. He asked dad if he could write out one or two letters recommending the ointment and to sign them with notable names of the day: Lady So and So, The Honourable Such and Such, and so on. Now the Scotsman was ready for the 'punters'. He sold the stuff at sixpence per box; according to him it could cure anything. You name it, this stuff could cure it. Over the weekend he sold the lot and made a handsome profit. Of course the stall holders weren't all like him; most of them were genuine dealers who gave value for money and lots of bargains.

One day, two of the local detectives called in for a drink and a chat. They were regular customers. One of them asked if my dad had any sovereigns in the till, saying it was his wife's birthday and he wanted a couple to give her for her birthday. Dad obliged by saying, "Yes, as a matter of fact I've taken a few this week, you can have them." That's when they pounced. They wanted to know who had changed them and when and at what time of day! It emerged that the chap who had changed the sovereigns was a painter and decorator and the firm he worked for had recently finished painting a house in Gosforth. He had been working in the house, and after the job was done had gone back and burgled the place, stealing a number of sovereigns. He was caught and sent to prison.

Ye Olde Plough was closed in 1933, they said through lack of facilities, toilets etc. My father then took over the management of the *Gloucester Inn*, Gateshead, for a man called Jack Robinson who also owned *The Wylam Hotel* in Gateshead. Jack Robinson lived privately in Low Fell and he had managers in both pubs. Jack was a typical self-made Gateshead businessman. Always wore a new flat cap; a quick talker and, whenever I saw him, he always gave me sixpence. Jack sold out to *McEwans Breweries* in 1934 but my father carried on managing the *Gloucester*.

In 1935 it was King George V and Queen Mary's Silver Jubilee. We entered a competition organised by the Gateshead Corporation for the best-decorated street. From Jackson Street up High West Street, there was Charles Street, Grahamsley Street 'our street' then Ann Street and Cuthbert Street. Everyone painted the front doors, windows and window-sills: red, white and blue. We had a massive carved wooden archway erected at the top of Grahamsley Street with bunting stretched across the street and all the way down the road. We didn't win the competition; Charles Street won, but we had a Jubilee tea with tables and trestles laid out down the middle of the street. Seventy-five per cent of the people living in Grahamsley Street were on the dole in 1935, so it was a great effort and sacrifice to put on such a show. Everyone mucked in to help and one man who worked as a window cleaner, took us all into 'Turners' sweet shop and general dealers, which was in the middle of Grahamsley Street, where he bought us all a penn'orth of sweets. The shop front had an old-fashioned bow window, and the last time I saw it, it was in the museum at Saltwell Park, Gateshead. I spent many a happy day in that park. It used to cost a ha'penny to go by tram car from Jackson Street to the terminus which was at the north entrance.

There was always such a wonderful display of flowers, trees and bushes which we never saw on High West Street; you could hire a rowing boat on the lake for tuppence; and fourpence for the gondolas, per hour: a little bit of paradise in the middle of Gateshead.

My sister, Dora, myself and my two cousins were often packed off to the Park for the day where we had a great time, getting home about 6 pm, dog tired. The pals that I can remember from those days were Jackie Monkhouse, who had an older sister called Mary, they lived in Arthur Street. Jackie was a studious sort of lad who liked painting and drawing, making models of aeroplanes etc. There was another lad called John Kent; he lived at the top of Grahamsley Street. I had a set of boxing gloves and he and I used to spar most nights after school. There were two rough lads in the street, one called Jackie Carter and the other, Tucker Huldey. They never went to the barbers; but had their heads shaved with the hand shears, leaving a little bob of hair on the brow.

We played football in the Quarry, a piece of waste land between Charles and Grahamsley Streets. As I was the only boy in the street who had a proper leather football, they would come and call on me to play and bring my ball. Occasionally my mother would call me in from the back window of the pub which overlooked the Quarry. She would shout: "Billy Boy, come and get your tea, dear." I used to hate this 'Billy Boy' stuff, as the lads took the mickey saying "Go on home for your tea, you little Jessie." When I asked to take my ball with me they refused to give it.

One particular night I came in for my tea looking glum. My dad said, "What's the matter with you then?" I told him the lads wouldn't give me my football back when I was called in. He'd had a few drinks in the afternoon, and said, "If they divvent give ye your baall back, get a hammer and hit them on the heed. They'll soon give ye your ball back."

After tea I complied with dad's wishes and on the way out I picked up a small hammer we used for breaking the coal, popped it in my pocket and went back to the Quarry'. I asked for the ball. They were still playing. Jackie Carter said: "Piss off."

I walked up to him and popped him on the head with the small hammer. There was a look of complete astonishment on his face. His eyes rolled back into his head and a pigeon-egg-sized lump came up on his shaven head as he crumpled at my feet. The rest of them ran away, so I picked up the football and went home. Jimmy Davison and Tucker Huldey went back and helped Jackie home. He was 'out' only a short while, but there was Hell on in the Street that night. Mrs Carter was going mad about her Jackie! After a time it all calmed down. My mother and Mrs Carter had a long chat and things were patched up. The lads never called me a 'little Jessie' again and Jackie Carter and I became great friends before we left Gateshead.

The Quarry yard was a place the show folk used as a winter

stopping place. After travelling the whole summer they came to the Quarry and set up their shows for the winter. It wasn't a large area. About twenty-five caravans would pull in and set up. The two main shows were *The Swish* and *The Steam Air Ships*. These were owned by the Hoadleys. Mrs Hoadley had a beautiful van, she also had two sons who ran the business. Tommy and Polly Caris always came with them. Tommy was in charge of assembling and maintaining the rides. The shows were on two nights per week, Friday and Saturday. Supporting the main attractions were all the sideshows with dart stalls: "three darts a penny" was the cry. You had to score 100 to win or hit three separate playing cards. There were circular stalls, where you had to roll your penny down a little wooden slide on to a board covered in painted squares, getting your penny exactly in the square to win whatever number of pennies was painted inside.

All the old names in the Travelling Business of the north were there: the Murphys, Millars, Richardsons, Turners, and Nobles. They all came to the Quarry.

There was one show next to the Coconut Shy called *Beat the Goalie*, a long narrow netted area with the goal post at the end. You had to kick the ball past the Goalie to win. The Millars ran that, and young Millar was the Goalie; they seldom beat him.

Dad used to organise charabanc trips for a Sunday morning run out. They called themselves *The Forty Club*, leaving Gateshead at about eight o'clock Sunday morning and getting back two o'clock Sunday afternoon. Dad did a 'reci' the week before to time the run. He always went with Joe and Annie Blakeborough and mam made the foursome, for their day off. Places like Corbridge or Hexham, Allendale, Morpeth, Rothbury and Warkworth were popular. They took the usual sandwiches and cases of beer on the charabanc and would occasionally stop for a drink at some small village pub.

One Sunday they pulled up at a village just west of Hexham. Now, forty men arriving unannounced at a small pub can be a little nerve-racking for the landlord. However, they were all served and settled in when Old Charlie Silversides, who was all for a bit of fun, called the Landlord up to the top of the counter, where he and his pal, my grandad were sitting. Charlie asked the landlord if he had anyone sitting up with the beer! "No, why?" replied the landlord. "Because," said Charlie, "they're sitting up with my old aunt and she's not half as bad as this beer!" The joke didn't go down well and they were all chucked out.

I still have the solid gold watch and chain with a gold medal attached which says 'Presented to William Kell for his kindness to the *Forty Club*, 1933',

Kell Jnr goes to the Dogs

Early in 1947 I was in the bar of the *Portland* talking and serving a friend who had just been demobbed from the 2nd Battalion of the Coldstream Guards. He was on his demob leave, by name of Tony Donahoe. Tony said he was going to visit a little place in Ireland called Belmullet in County Mayo. His parents came from there to Ashington when they were first married and he wanted to take this opportunity to visit the place and meet some of his Irish relatives. He asked if I would like to make the trip with him. It sounded interesting and I said, "OK, I'll go."

So everything was arranged; tickets and a travel permit for me and, as a civilian, I needed a travel permit from the Ministry of Labour. I had never been abroad. I was twenty years old and knew nothing about life or travel! I treated the whole thing as an adventure.

We set off early in February. The journey from Newcastle to Holyhead took about ten hours by train. There had been heavy storms and flooding, and the departure of the ferry was delayed for the arrival of the London train. It was a choppy crossing of the Irish Sea and we arrived in Dublin on the train from Dun Laoghaire at 1.00 am without any accommodation booked. Because of the delayed crossing, the Catholic Women's League had a small desk on the platform where you could go and arrange lodgings for the night. We ended up in a boarding house, somewhere near Allanstown Park. The next day was Sunday and there were no buses running to Belmullet so we had to stay over in Dublin till Monday. That gave us time to have a look around Dublin's fair city. There was no rationing in Ireland and the shops were full of food, clothes and things we hadn't seen since before the war.

Our first breakfast in Dublin consisted of two fried eggs, three rashers of bacon, three sausages, tomatoes and toast with as much butter as you wanted. What a feed! We caught the noon bus from Dublin to Ballina which is right across Ireland from east to west.

At each small town we stopped for a short while to allow the passengers to get off, or on, with all sorts of luggage and all sorts of livestock. When we were about to leave, someone would get on to the bus – a boy or girl – and they would sing a song or play the fiddle or a small accordion for us, then go around with the hat for a collection.

We arrived in Ballina about tea time and found that we had to wait for the bus to Belmullet which was to go at nine o'clock. We had a lovely tea in a small café just opposite the bus station, and spent the rest of the time having a look around the town. We had a few Irish whiskeys to warm us for the journey and eventually boarded the bus. An old lady got on the bus and as she walked past me she looked me straight in the eye and started calling me all the names she could think of. I had never seen her before and I got quite a shock at her behaviour, but this was Ireland! I just looked down at the floor and kept quiet.

The bus driver dropped us off at Tony's cousin's place and they were all waiting to meet us. It was a smallholding called 'Achicanune', about three quarters of a mile out of Belmullet. A typical Mayo smallholding house, living room in the middle and a bedroom at each end, with a peat fire for heating, cooking, boiling and baking in the living room. There was no bathroom or toilet. You washed in a bowl with water from a jug which was brought from the hand pump outside. I asked Tony, "What do you do when you want to go?"

He said, "Use the hemmel across the road or go down the hedge." Well! The hemmel had three young heifers in that were very curious each time you went in, and if it was night time the wind blew your candle out. Down the hedge wasn't very comfortable as it was February, and the gales were lashing in from the Atlantic. It also sometimes blew your paper away! After a few days of this my asthma started playing up and the doctor was called. He diagnosed *Asian Flu* and wanted me isolated in a private room in Belmullet Hospital. So off I went to hospital: a Trust Hospital, financed by the Irish Sweepstake Lottery. They were very kind to me and the Sister in charge had been on the bus the night I was told off by the old lady. She said, "I remember you looked most embarrassed." I was treated like a lord, with my own private room, toilet and bathroom facilities and for six days I had the best of food and attention.

The doctor's name was Dr Bryne and he called to see me every day and stayed and talked about cars, which seemed to be his hobby. I told him I had a *Singer* 9HP overhead camshaft which was fast and economical. He liked to sit and talk about all sorts of subjects and invited me to come back and stay with him in June as the fishing was excellent in Belmullet then. I was sorry to leave the hospital after six days; they had all been so nice to me.

While I was in hospital Tony had been busy organising things. Each morning we walked down to the village and called into *McLoughlin's Hotel* for our 'ablutions': a wash and brush up, etc. Then we ordered breakfast: wonderful home-cured ham and eggs. Then we'd either visit some of Tony's relatives or hire the only taxi in the village and go sight seeing for the day. The taxi was American: an old *Studebaker*, well sprung, with a most eccentric Irishman driving. He knew all the local history and gossip and he only drank Hennessey *Three Star* brandy. Tony mentioned that we might be interested in buying a good racing greyhound.

"Sure," said the taxi driver, "and couldn't I be taking you to see the best greyhound breeder in County Mayo. He's a man called Donavan Fitzpatrick who has a village pub in Black Sod Bay, just a few miles up the coast." We said we would arrange to go and see him. It was arranged for the following week, and we left it all to the taxi driver to pick us up and take us.

In the meantime, Tony's relatives were organising parties and dances in different houses to welcome us to Ireland. At one of these dances I met a pretty girl called Nellie Coyle. She had honey-blond hair and bright green eyes. I told her I wasn't much good at doing the local dances, jigs and reels. But Nellie said she would teach me. We got on quite well and she was very friendly. I asked if she would be going to a Party Dance arranged for our welcome in the village hall in Belmullet. Nellie said she worked in her father's butchers shop and would be late arriving at the dance, but she would definitely be there.

On the night of the village dance, everyone for miles around was there. Tony and I had a great time. Most of the people were his relatives. Nellie turned up and we danced most of the time together. I asked her what she did with her free time. She said she went dancing with the village crowd, and liked walking. She was preparing to go to England to work as a nurse in St Alban's Hospital in the near future. I asked to meet her the following night. She said, "OK, I'll meet you in church at 9 pm." I thought she was joking. But sure enough the following night I went around to the small Catholic Church at 9 pm and there she was, sitting three rows from the back of the church wearing a silk headscarf.

When she saw me she got up into the aisle, knelt down on one knee, facing the Altar, made the sign of the cross, turned around and came out of the church. When she came out I asked her, "Why the Church?"

She said, "It is the only place in the village to meet you. I wouldn't meet you in a pub nor on the street. Too many people might see us and it wouldn't be right." In other words she would feel compromised. I thought what a funny old place Ireland is.

We walked through the village. She showed me her father's butcher's shop and where she lived. We talked about what we were going to do with our lives. She was determined to be a nurse in England, as there was nothing for her in Belmullet. I promised to visit her when she came to England. The time I spent in Belmullet we became good friends, and after I got back home we wrote to each other once or twice. She used to send me parcels of meat with spices in to preserve it, as meat was still rationed at home. She certainly had dignity that girl – I never visited her when she came to England. I let her down. Sorry, Nellie.

The day came around for the trip to Black Sod Bay and we were met outside *McLoughlin's Hotel* by the eccentric taxi driver just after lunch. It was a rough ride. The road was potholed and, with the taxi being well sprung, we were well shaken when we arrived at the greyhound breeder's place. Mr Fitzpatrick was a retired Police Sergeant who had spent nearly thirty years as a policeman in Bournemouth of which he was very proud. He had retired, come home, and bought the business in Black Sod Bay. It was a General Dealers and a pub all in one. The greyhound breeding was a hobby with him.

We were made very welcome. The taxi driver had let him know we were coming. He invited us to try his 'porter' *Guinness* which we enjoyed. And his married daughter had arranged tea for us. We talked about Tony's relatives, Bournemouth and greyhounds; the afternoon passed very pleasantly. Mr Fitzpatrick took us out to see the only greyhound puppy he had left for sale. It was a fawn brindle bitch, eight months old, and bred from two champions. Her sire was *Rebel Light* who had been coursing champion and her dam had been a record breaker at Allanstown Park in Dublin. Her name was *Allanstown Lady*.

Tony and I decided to buy the bitch as soon as we saw her, and we paid £40 for her, cash. Mr Fitzpatrick said he would arrange to send her by rail and ship to Ashington for us, and not to worry about her as he had been sending dogs to England for years. With the deal all settled, we arranged to have the greyhound sent to us a few weeks after we were due back home. We decided to call 'our' greyhound *Allan's Light*.

Back in Belmullet it was parties and get-togethers every night. One of Tony's cousins, called John Joe Barrett, nineteen years old was a fine fiddle player. He played at most of the dances and gatherings we went to. A grand lad, full of life, curly brown hair, rosy-cheeked and always smiling. I think he enjoyed our visit as much as we did. He was going with a bonny dark-haired girl, and we often walked home together after the parties. I asked him one time where did he do his courting, as there was nowhere in Belmullet to take a girl, other than the two pubs.

He said, "Have you noticed those piles of peat stacked at intervals along the side of the roads? They're shaped like the roof of a house, and they're stacked like that to dry out."

I said, "Yes, I'd noticed."

He said, "Well, the local lads and lasses make a small hole in the end of the peat stacks and crawl in. There's room for two inside and it's nice and warm on winter nights. And that's where some of us do our courting, after the dances."

I used to listen to the songs they sang. We often had a sing song in *McLoughlin's* and the other little pub across the square. It was owned by an old lady, I forget her name, but she had a girl who managed the pub for her, a small fair-haired girl, always looking for business and eager to please. The lads used to ask her to sing us a song. Sometimes she would oblige, and I remember only the chorus of one song she sang, it went like this:

> *Knock on my window tonight, love*
> *Knock on it gently and light, love*
> *Knock on my window tonight, love*
> *For it's there I'll be waiting for you.*

A real Irish ditty. *Patsy Fagan* was another favourite when we could all join in with the chorus. Belmullet was the first place I noticed drinkers putting cordial in their beer. It was unheard of in

Ashington in 1947. County Mayo has a beauty all of its own, even in February, I'm glad I went there.

It was getting near the time to leave Belmullet, and Tony suggested we buy some food to take home with us: cured ham, butter, tea etc. Tony had his cut and parcelled into one-pound packets for easy packing. I decided to buy a ham for my mother, twelve or fourteen pounds. I had to buy a suitcase to put it in and I was assured that I would get it through customs.

I carried it across Ireland, right to the docks at Dun Laoghaire and into the customs shed. Tony went through the 'Forces Only' customs section. I was stopped and my cases searched. He was a small man, the customs officer, and when I opened the case with the ham, his eyes lit up. "Have you got an Export Licence for this ham?" he said.

"No," I replied, "I didn't know you needed one. It's a present for my mother."

He lifted the ham out of the case and pushed it under the counter, saying, "If we allow everyone to take food out of the country like this we'll have nothing left to eat ourselves. I'm confiscating it! What's your name and address?"

That was the last I saw of my ham. Tony got through with everything he bought; they didn't bother with members of the Forces.

Back home in Ashington I settled down to my job again. Meanwhile, Tony got fixed up with a job at Ashington Colliery. About a month after we got back home we received a telegram from Mr Fitzpatrick to say he had travelled to Dublin with the greyhound and put her on the ship himself. She duly arrived at Ashington Railway Station, looking very forlorn – it's a hell of a journey. We picked her up and brought her to the *Portland* where we had a kennel ready.

Tony and I knew nothing about training greyhounds. So we had to take advice, and that came from *all* directions. First she had to be walked at a brisk pace for ten miles every day, Tony and I would take this in shifts. I would do the morning shift, he would do evenings. This would depend on what shift Tony was working at the pit. My shift would take me and 'Meg' down through Ashington to Newbiggin, via Woodhorn Pit, along the narrow path to Newbiggin, which came out at Newbiggin Railway Station. On the return journey we came back via North Seaton Village and up through the Hirst and back to the *Portland*. That would be about eight miles.

Tony's stint would be the other way out of Ashington, up by Douglas' farm and down the path to the River Wansbeck and along Sheepwash Bridge, up Sheepwash Bank and home via Cooper's Shop at the top end of Ashington. We did this every day for nearly a year until 'Meg' was eighteen months old. We also had to register her with The Kennel Club and The Greyhound Racing Club which meant she had to have a registered identity card with all her markings identified.

Tony and I had decided to race her at Brough Park, Newcastle which was run under NGRC rules. We went in to see the Manager of Brough Park, a Mr Burrows. He explained what was required of us and if we signed the acceptance form he would place the dog with one of his trainers, a Mr Thompson. We agreed, and signed, and arranged to take the greyhound in for a trial run before Mr Thompson would accept her. We knew she was fast because we had tried her against a bunch of Billy Ferrell's greyhounds with the old fashioned 'rabbit skin' on a string, wound around a bicycle wheel, on the turf of Newbiggin Golf Course. She had beaten all four of Billy's best dogs by yards. I remember Billy's face that afternoon. He looked as sick as a dog. I nearly cracked that old one about 'running away from them' but he looked so miserable I hadn't the heart.

Mr Thompson was satisfied with the trial and said he would take her for training. He said that once she went into the kennels we would have no contact with her, as that was the rule of the stadium. We were kept informed of her progress. And when she was having her training track runs, usually in the morning about eleven o'clock, we went through to Brough Park to see how she was developing. Within six weeks she had improved one hundred per cent. Under professional handling her muscles developed all over her frame, and she was trapping perfectly. We were told she would be tried in a Novice Race on the following week. It would be about six hundred yards. Thompson told us she could have a chance to win, but he thought the Number One dog was too strong for her. So on the night of the race – a Wednesday night meeting – Tony and I had a few pounds on her and a few pounds on 'The Red' as a saver. Alan's Light won by about twenty lengths at four to one. What a thrill! What a climax to all that walking, and all that hard work.

Over the next few weeks she ran another five races, winning three and coming second twice. Each time she ran Mr Thompson would say the same thing: she had a chance to win but some other 'bloody' dog would probably beat her. What information! Each time she won they kept moving her up a class and obviously it became harder for her to win. Then, with moving her up in class races, the distance was farther, to six hundred and twenty-five yards. Those last twenty-five yards were too much for her, that's how she was beaten into second place on two occasions.

One night, just after she had won her race, Tony and I were approached by another greyhound owner who offered us two hundred pounds for her. He said, "If I take her to Sunderland she'll break the record there." Sunderland was a shorter track and it would suit her much better.

Tony and I thought about it for a minute or two. I said, "If she can break the track record at Sunderland for you, she can do it for us just as well. No sale."

One week later she 'broke down', came into season and was unable to race. We wanted to bring her home, but we were advised to leave her at Brough Park where she would be well looked after and kept in good shape, ready to race after she had dried up.

About two weeks later I received a 'phone call from Mr Burrows the Manager of Brough Park, informing me that *Allan's Light* had disappeared from her kennel and was missing. Had we seen anything of her?

No, we hadn't seen her and how could that happen?

They didn't know how she had got out. There had been another greyhound in the kennel with her and that was still there.

We smelt a rat. We put an advertisement in the papers offering a reward for her return. We told the Newcastle Police who had already been informed by Brough Park. We were visited by a CID man from Hedlam Street Police Station – he was no help; didn't seem to be interested. Days and weeks went by and no sign of her. We decided to go and see Mr Burrows to claim compensation for the loss of our greyhound. We 'phoned him and arranged a meeting. He met us in his office at Brough Park, and on his desk was the agreement we had signed. He pointed out to us that, by signing, we had agreed Brought Park was under no obligation for the welfare or loss of our greyhound. No obligation! Even to the neglect of the greyhound. That was in the small print.

We didn't get a penny for our dog and we never saw her again. As far as I was concerned that was the end of greyhounds for me.

I took a philosophical view of the loss of our dog. I didn't want to get into gambling. I liked the thrill of the chase, and the beauty of the racing greyhounds, but I didn't want to get hooked on gambling.

My dad told me a tale about his experience at a pitch and toss school which was held at Heworth, alongside the old Heworth Colliery Railway line. A crowd of men had gathered there to gamble on the toss of two pennies in the air; if they came down heads you won. If they came down a head and a tail you had another go, but if you got two tails you lost.

Dad was sitting on the embankment smoking a *Woodbine* waiting for the game to break up, so that he could get a handout from the eventual winner. My dad had tailed them for £40. Another man, his face as white as a sheet, came and sat beside him. He had also tailed them for £20, a lot of money in those days. My dad offered him a *Woodbine.* He took one but he never got it lit. This fella started to make deep ruttling sounds in his throat and fell back, dead. My dad shouted to the rest of the men: "this bloke's snuffed it!"

There was a hell of a scramble and they all ran away down the railway line, leaving my dad with the dead man. What could he do? It was against the law to play pitch and toss. And he couldn't do anything for the dead man. So he ran as fast as he could along the railway line, two sleepers at a time, and didn't stop until he arrived at Felling station.

Tony Donahoe was upset about the loss of the dog, and he decided to go back to Ireland and have a look at some more greyhounds. He asked if I was interested, but I decided greyhounds were not for me.

The *Portland*'s post-war Characters

1947 was my 21st year, a good year. My dad had promised to buy me an MG sports car for my '21st' if I worked hard in the pub. So just before my birthday I went to Billy Gibson's garage in High Market, Ashington, and filled in an order form for a red MG sports car. They were in short supply with a waiting list of three years, but I ordered it anyway. I had a little car of my own, a *Singer* 9 HP which I used according to the petrol ration, not a lot. About four gallons per month.

With all the walking and training of the dog I was extremely fit, and I kept in trim with running and weight training and a bit of boxing. I boxed with Jackie Bell who had just been demobbed from the Navy. He was a 'canny hand' at boxing and we both enjoyed our sessions twice a week in the big room upstairs in the *Portland*.

I also liked going to the local dances. I wasn't a good dancer – but I managed. I was just learning to dance, at the *Princess Ballroom* in Ashington, when it burned down. The date was 4.4.44, an easy date to remember. The *Princess* was one of the finest ballrooms in the North East, built as a ballroom with a sprung floor and all the facilities. It was a great loss to Ashington at that time.

Dryden Phillipson was the Band Leader at the beginning of the war. He was called up and Harry Hogarth took over from him. Harry was always very smart and upright; he played the piano. A good Band Leader. He had a local girl as vocalist. Her name was Connie Allsopp. What a wonderful voice she had. With the right guidance she could have reached the top.

One night at the *Princess*, the dance was going well; the place was packed, when Harry Hogarth stopped the band to make an announcement:

"*The British 8th Army has retaken Bizerta.*" There was a huge cheer from the whole crowd.

After the *Princess* burnt down there was only the Co-op Arcade Hall that was available for dancing, which was two floors up above the Co-op Department Store. Not quite the same!

In the immediate travelling area there was the *Clayton* Dance Hall at Bedlington Station which could be reached very easily by bus or train, similar to the *Roxy* Ballroom at Blyth.

Some of the Big Bands of the time played the *Roxy*, for one night stands: Joe Loss, Oscar Rabin, Eric Whinstone and Nat Gonella. The resident Band leader was Tommy Bell, a popular man with the local dancing crowd.

My job limited my social activities, as I worked until 10 pm six nights a week. Wednesday was my usual day off, and nothing much happened on Wednesdays.

If I pushed it I could make it to the *Arcade* for 10.30 pm on dance nights. The dances ended at 11 pm so I never got in a lot of dancing. From the *Portland* to the *Arcade* was just over a mile. Without the car, it wasn't worth going – unless I ran all the way. I usually made it to the dance as most of the girls were on their way out. One night I was in a hurry to get to the dance. I had to sweep up the bar before I could go so I was brushing around the feet of the customers, hinting to them that I wanted them out. My dad called to me and said, in front of the men that were left standing at the bar, "You're in a hell of a hurry, Bill. You know you haven't invented sex. It's been around a long time. Oh, leave the brush and gerraway to the dance!" The men all started to laugh. My face was red.

There were some 'bonny' girls in Ashington who were friends of mine: Marjorie Watson was a dark-eyed beauty, one of my first girl friends; Lucy Bell was a beautifully bronzed blonde with hair bleached by the Northumbrian sun. She had a tanned skin, with working outdoors as a Land Army girl, and worked on the Ashington Coal Company farms. I saw her every day, cycling up past the *Portland* on her way to and from work. I met her through going to the *Arcade* dance and we became real good pals. She lived in one of the streets in the Hirst, and if I had the car, I used to take her home. I met her mam and dad – 'canny folks'. Her mam was a pretty woman with dark hair and kind eyes. Lucy married a pal of mine, George Strong. I think they had three sons, but I'm not sure.

Pat Pollard was another dancing partner, one of three very attractive sisters. Pat was a strikingly beautiful little, dark-haired, dark-eyed girl. We had some good times together. We enjoyed life.

Hilda Riches was another ultra smart girl. The first time I saw her in her Wren's uniform, she looked like a model advert for recruitment to the Navy. I liked her, we got on well together. She was tall and honey blonde with a great sense of humour. She married an Ashington lad and they have one son.

I used to knock about with a bunch of mates, most of them musicians: Les Stevenson played the guitar; Alex Cummings, sax and clarinet; Alex's cousin John Lamb played drums; Billy Green from Morpeth, played the piano; Percy Jobson from Morpeth, played the bass fiddle; Dick Slaughter, played the piano. We had some grand musical nights together, all good pals.

I was also great friends with some of the lads who came from Hebburn to work at *Reyrolles* Factory in Ashington. Eric Quinn was best man at my wedding and Billy Corrigan who I played football with for *Reyrolles* team. They all came to the *Portland* for a drink, and we were all good friends, as was a lad called Alex Watson. His father and mine had been friends when they were young men in Newcastle. His father had come to Ashington to work as a boss for the *North Eastern Electricity Company* about the same time as my dad came to Ashington, so we were family friends.

Alex was a Junior Engineer in the Merchant Navy on the cargo ship *Vernon City* when she was torpedoed in the South Atlantic on 28th June, 1943. The crew took to the boats as the ship sank. Alex was in a lifeboat with 12 other crew including the Captain. Just after the ship sank, a German 'U-Boat' surfaced alongside the lifeboat and a monacled U-Boat Commander spoke to them from the conning tower of the submarine. His first words to them, in perfect English were: "The fortunes of war, gentlemen. I would like your Captain to come aboard for interrogation." The Captain of the *Vernon City* went aboard the U-Boat and later was put back into the lifeboat. The U-Boat Commander told them he could give them water, but had no food to spare. They were given water and cut adrift, and the U-Boat submerged.

Alex told me when the U-Boat dived he had never felt so lonely in his life. Their Captain said: "Well lads, the nearest land to us from here is Brazil." So he set a course for the nearest landfall. The crew took turns at rowing, for seven days and seven nights and eventually landed on a beach near a small fishing village. They were helped by the Brazilian fishermen who were kind to them. Alex was in a very poor condition. His tongue had swollen so much it was sticking out of his mouth and his legs bulged to twice their size through lack of water and exposure to the sun and salt water. He was nursed and looked after by one of the Brazilian fishermen's families. They had little to eat themselves but they gave him all they had and were most kind to him. He was twenty at the time, and he said he has always been very grateful to them for all they did for him.

The Brazilian Authorities eventually sent him and the rest of the crew to New York where they were housed in a hotel run by the British Merchant Navy until they could be shipped back home. They were given free hotel accommodation, but very little money. So while Alex was in New York he took a job as a carpet salesman in one of the big stores.

The Merchant Navy lads were treated well by the New Yorkers, who would call at the hotel and take them home for a meal or a night out on the town. Alex was taken one night to Eddie Cantor's New York apartment and made very welcome. They were all hospitable to the lads. Alex, after a three months wait, got a post on a Manchester Liner, the *Pacific Exporter* and arrived in Manchester on 21st September, 1943. That U-Boat Commander certainly impressed Alex, and he vowed when he was rescued he would learn to speak German. He now speaks German fluently. His wife Betty learned and speaks German too.

In the summers of '47 and '48 when Alex came on leave after a long spell at sea, we would go down to Newbiggin for the day, parking the car at the *Old Ship Inn*. We'd go in for lunch and then go down to the beach and hire a rowing boat from one of the old fishermen. The charge was ten shillings, for the day, and Alex and I would spend the rest of the afternoon just rowing about Newbiggin Bay, fishing, swimming or just sunbathing in the boat. They were old fashioned summers in those days. Long warm summers; most enjoyable.

The pubs were going extremely well. Yet there were still shortages and beer was allocated to you on your pre-war sales. We could sell all we could get, but our allocation was only 8 Hogsheads of beer. That's 54 gallons per Hogshead; and about 40 dozen bottled beers including *Guinness*. Our spirits quota was generous. That came once a month, but it never lasted more than a fortnight.

The spirit delivery usually came about the third or fourth day of the month and most of our regular spirit drinkers would call in and be courteous and nice to my father, to find out if the delivery had been made, because the spirits were never displayed, but kept under the counter and mainly dispensed by my father.

The whisky was kept under the counter at the top of the bar, near the fireplace, where my father always stood. The spirits were rationed out to everyone under his strict supervision. Some of the names I remember were Joe Johnson, the baker; and his pal, Percy Clough, the piano player; Percy Cawthorne, the Chemist; and Phil Storey who lived in the Seventh Row just across from the *Portland*. We had an off sales section, called the 'Bottle and Jug' which held eight stools, four on each side. And we had our regulars in there every night: old Mrs Simpson, and there were *three* Mrs Thompsons and a number of others. It was a woman's domain and men were only endured under duress. The women sat and talked while enjoying their bottle of *Guinness* and occasional 'short'. For entertainment, Mrs Thompson would go into a trance and bring them messages back from their 'dead' husbands. There were two Mrs Turnbulls. One was from Bothal Village; a tall dark woman of striking beauty, who would be in her fifties then. She came into the Bottle and Jug on her own for a drink after being to see a film at one of our five Picture Halls in Ashington at that time. Another Mrs Turnbull was a 'canny old soul' who was a regular. She had a married daughter, a Mrs Thompson whose daughter is now Ashington's 'Glamorous Grandma' herself: Mrs May Summers. 'All canny folk'.

In June 1948 some of my pals and myself booked to go to Butlins in Pwllheli, Wales for our holidays. These were George Nichol, Doug Scott, Winston Ball, Jackie Tweddle, Alex Cummings, Les Stevenson and myself.

Les and I went in my car with most of our luggage, and the rest of the lads went on motor bikes.

We set off early on the Saturday morning to meet at Butlins about lunchtime. Les and I took turns at driving, but it took much longer than we thought to get to our destination. By lunchtime we were still miles from Pwllheli. We became worried because we were carrying Doug Scott's medication for his diabetes. He had to have an injection of insulin regularly. We arrived eventually in the late afternoon and Doug was fine.

On the Monday I went down with tonsilitis and was confined to bed for three days by the Camp doctor. However, I soon recovered and got back into the swing of things.

The lads were thoroughly enjoying themselves; plenty to do, all sorts of entertainment and sports, plenty of girls. Ideally designed for a bunch of young lads.

We all entered on behalf of our 'House' whichever sport we thought we were best at. Roy Stuart was also with us and he was a professional Foot Runner. He ran under the name of 'Hall of Linton'. He entered and won most of the foot races.

Working at the camp as a Redcoat was a lad from Whitley Bay; his name was Irvine Kaye who helped organise most of the sporting activities on the camp. He 'palled up' with us, as we were fellow Geordies. Irvine knew the run of the camp and the surrounding countryside and he was a great help in making our holiday a success. He got to know that I was interested in boxing so he entered Roy and me for the boxing competition for the campers. All you had to do was fill in a form with your name, age, weight and height and the name of the 'House' you represented. The Redcoats sorted the rest out. Roy was drawn against another camper and I was drawn against the camp boxing instructor, a short well-built man who had been a PTI in the Army. Roy won his fight, then it was my turn. A Redcoat acted as referee and when he called us into the middle of the ring he said to me, "Just put up a good show, he won't hurt you."

There were three rounds to the match. The first round went well and we were applauded by the crowd on going back to our corners. I was a little more confident in the second round and it went well for me, I thought, as we went back to our corners for the second time. When we came out for the third and last round to shake hands, the PTI said to me, "I'm sorry, son, I can't let you win. It's more than my job's worth." He gave me a boxing lesson; also a split lip and a painful red ear. I lost, but I was applauded for my effort. I enjoyed having a go and the lads were all proud of me.

Irvine Kaye borrowed a guitar from one of his Redcoat friends and Les Stevenson used it to accompany the lads in a sing song whenever we felt like it. Alex Cummings would sing *The Lambton Worm* and we'd all join in the chorus. I sang *Patsy Fagan* and the lads joined in, singing their heads off.

On the Friday night of the second week it was 'farewell night' for the campers and our last night too. After dinner we all met in the Ballroom for a party. The resident orchestra for that season was Eric Whinston, who wrote that evergreen tune *Stagecoach*. Eric's orchestra was one of the top bands in the country at that time, very professional. Alex, Les and Winston were intrigued by the band, being musicians themselves, and they socialised well with the band lads.

Towards the end of the evening I noticed a pretty dark-haired girl standing near the dance floor, on her own. I plucked up the courage to go over and ask her for a dance. She said "yes" and we got up on the dance floor. She was small, only about 5 feet 3 inches tall, but quite smart and trim. To open the conversation I said "I've noticed you once or twice around the camp this week."

She came straight back with the reply, "I've noticed you too. I saw you in the boxing ring."

I asked her to come and join our farewell party, which she did, as she was leaving the following day too. The party was a huge success. Everyone enjoyed themselves. We exchanged addresses the following morning when she came around to see us off. She was getting a lift home in a car with some friends. She came from the steel town, Corby, and her name was Adams. I wonder where she is now? I never saw her again.

Les and I enjoyed a leisurely trip home. The countryside of North Wales was beautiful that June. We came up through Portmadoc, Betws-y-coed, and on up through Chester, towards Preston and across country over the moors to the old A1 and then home. There were no motorways in those days. A memorable two weeks.

In 1948 supplies were beginning to improve and the pub business was doing well. There was no shortage of jobs and the lads coming out of the Forces had plenty of money to spend. All the Ashington pits were working at full capacity. The pub was full every night and packed at weekends. Sunday night was quiet because the twenty-two clubs in Ashington were allowed music and concert parties and we were only allowed Radio or as we called it the 'Wireless'. But we still had a hard core of regulars coming in on Sunday night, and everyone knew everyone else. They all had their regular seats and there was a real friendly atmosphere. We got away with music on a Sunday morning by forming a Jolly Boys Club. Buck Milburn and Jimmy Bacon played the piano and drums and one of the lads acted as concert chairman. All the members had to get up and do a turn, either sing, whistle or recite. Some were good. Some were bloody awful; but they were all given a fair hearing and were always applauded with honest appreciation.

There were some good local talent: Donnie Allsopp, the brother of Connie, was an entertaining singer, medium-sized, fair-haired young lad. When he sang *Are you Lonesome Tonight* it brought the tears streaming down the older women's faces. Jimmy Bacon had a good strong voice and his *Bless this House* always had the best of order.

Jimmy Coombs was a trained singer with a wonderful tenor voice; when he sang everyone put down their drinks. He brought a bit of culture into the proceedings. Buck Milburn had a following who liked to sing to his piano accompaniment. He could make an average singer sound great. Buck taught me how to put a song over. He even made me sound good at times. His cousin, Jackie Milburn, who was playing football for Newcastle United at that time, used to come into the *Portland* on a Sunday morning to listen to Buck play. Jackie was the local hero to the lads and he was always given a grand welcome when he came into the pub.

One Sunday morning Jackie and I arranged to go and see Buck's concert party who were booked to appear that night at the *Beamish Social Club*. We set off in my car and arrived at the club about 8.30 pm. We introduced ourselves to the doorman, an old man who had obviously been told by Buck that Wor Jackie was coming. He made us welcome and signed us both in. The concert party was performing in a large upstairs room which was packed. Jimmy Bacon was in the middle of singing *Bless this House* when Jackie put his head around the door to take a look. When the club members saw him there was a great roar, followed by clapping, whistling and shouting. Poor Jimmy's song was drowned out with all the noise. What a wonderful welcome. The committee had laid on a buffet supper and drinks for us. They were so pleased to see Jackie. We had a great night. The concert party included a girl called Pauline who sang popular ballads. She was Buck's sister-in-law. There was also Donnie Allsopp who liked to sing Al Jolson numbers, and an Ashington comedian whose name was George Meredith, one of the best local comics. Very talented, all of them.

In the Autumn of '48 a startlingly beautiful redheaded girl called into the pub with her mother for a drink. It was after a trip to the pictures. I had only seen her once before when she was in ATS uniform, obviously home on leave. She and her mother were always friendly when they called once or twice a week, and I always gave them every attention. I had occasion to call into the Morpeth Tax office to get my tax sorted out when to my surprise this same girl came to the counter to attend to me. She took great interest in my enquiries and sorted my problem out. Father and myself having the same name 'William' and working at the same address had been confusing to the Taxman. However, she put things right and I thanked her.

She smiled and said "That's OK. Anything to oblige."

The next time I saw her, I was taking delivery of our ration of cigarettes which were sent by *United* bus from Purvis's of Morpeth. I had the car parked outside the office at Ashington Bus Station and was busy loading the parcels of cigarettes into the car when a bus pulled slowly past going out of the station. I looked up and there she was, sitting directly above me. She looked down at me and gave me a beautiful smile as the bus pulled out. I would have given anything in the world to have leapt aboard that bus. But it was gone. It was 7 pm and I had to deliver the cigarettes to the *Portland* and get back to work behind the bar. What a life.

One night, a week or two later, Syd Ross came into the buffet bar and asked me if I would like to buy a ticket for his works dance which was to be held at the Morpeth Town Hall. He worked for *Swinneys* of Morpeth. I said I wasn't all that keen on dances at Morpeth. Then he told me that he had tried to sell a ticket to a nice redhead who travelled to Morpeth on the bus with him. She had told him that she had just come out of the ATS and didn't know anyone to go with.

Syd had said "Surely you know someone in Ashington?" She replied that she knew me slightly and might buy a ticket if *I* was going. What a salesman! I bought one immediately. Syd said "Now I might sell Rusty a ticket." I told him I would be working till 10 pm so I wouldn't get to his dance until after then. Syd said he would pass on the message.

I arrived at the dance just after ten and looked around to see if Rusty had turned up. She had, and she was dancing with someone. My heart sank. I didn't know him. However, faint heart never won fair lady. When the dance ended I went over and said "hello" and asked for the next dance.

Rusty said "yes" and we danced the next few dances together. I asked if she would let me take her home – and she agreed. The chap she had been with didn't give up that easily. He kept coming back for another dance during the course of the evening, but got the message, eventually. Thank God for Syd Ross.

We came home from Morpeth the long way round, and talked a lot. I couldn't believe she could be interested in me. She was so beautiful, bright, intelligent; I couldn't believe my luck. From that night we spent all the free time we had together. Rusty was a brilliant dancer so we went dancing as often as we could. My job was a bit of a bind, working till ten each night and every weekend, while Rusty had a 9 to 5 tax office job. But we had to put up with it. Rusty lived in Number 42 Fourth Row at the top end of Ashington. Her mam and dad were very understanding and allowed me to see her after I had finished work. Sometimes we went for a run in the car after I'd finished, just to be on our own.

We went down to Druridge Bay a lot, walking along the shore together, especially when it was quiet with no one else about. Another favourite place of ours was the village of Bothal. We'd park the car near the Vicar's house and walk down past the church, sometimes calling in. It's a beautiful little church, well worth a call. Then on down past the ramparts of Bothal Castle to the stepping stones across the river Wansbeck. Above the stones is a very narrow suspended footbridge which takes you to some well-kept market gardens at the base of the hillside. A bonny village is Bothal.

Rusty and I had two totally different family backgrounds. She had four brothers and two sisters. Her dad worked at Ashington pit as a day-shift worker, on a small wage, and her mam had her work cut out to make ends meet. My family consisted of one sister, Dora, and myself. My parents worked together in the pub and considered themselves well off. Rusty and I had a lot to learn about each other. Rusty's dad had been a member of the Ashington Branch of the Miners' Union during the 1920s and up until after the war. He was an active union man and a member of the Communist Party. The working conditions of the miners during this period were abysmal and James Mann, Rusty's dad, had much to fight for. He was a thorn in the side of the Ashington Coal Company and sometimes also an embarrassment to the union branch themselves. He fought for the rights of the Ashington miners, doing a lot of good work for men who had been injured in pit accidents; filling in forms and helping them to claim for their injuries.

He was also an active member of the Club and Institute Union where he was secretary of the *Central Club* for many years. A busy man.

Communists were as unpopular then as they are today. And my father, being a staunch 'Churchillian' didn't quite see eye-to-eye with Jimmy's politics. Rusty and I decided to keep them discreetly apart, at all times.

Just after opening time one morning, in the spring of 1949, a customer came in for a drink. After I had served him he said "some lucky lad is getting a brand new MG sports car. A bright red one. Gibson's garage lads were helping to unload it at the station depot as I came past. There's about a hundred people standing on the Station Bridge, watching them unload it off a low-loader railway wagon."

I didn't say anything at the time, but I thought *"I wonder if that could be mine?"*

Sure enough, later that day, I received a phone call from Bill Gibson. He said "We've got your car and are just checking it. It should be ready in a couple of days, then you can come up and collect it. The price is £620 on the road."

After I put the phone down, I started to think how I should approach my father to tell him my car had eventually arrived.

The astonished look on my dad's face told me all! "What? £620 for a bloody perambulator with two seats! No, you'll have to find your own money to pay for that."

What a let down after waiting so long for the car to be delivered. And he had *promised* to pay for it. I didn't get much sleep that night, wracking my brains to think how I could scrape up the money to pay for the car. After lunch the following day I told my mother what dad had said.

"That's just like him," she exploded. "I knew he wouldn't pay for it. Gan into the bedroom and get me bag. Aa'll pay for it."

I went for her handbag, a large one with a handle on the top just like a Bank cash bag.

"How much is it?"

"Six hundred and twenty pounds," I said.

My mother counted out the notes, put an elastic band around them and said "Now take that up to Gibson's and pay for the car."

I took the money up to the garage and saw Bill Gibson. When I handed him the money he said "You're a lucky lad, Bill. That's the first MG sports car we've had delivered since the war ended. Come through and have a look at it. My brother-in-law has gone to Moot Hall to register it, and we'll have her ready for you tomorrow morning."

I went to see *my* car: cherry red with silver-spoked wheels and cream-coloured leather upholstery. I felt great. It was a dream come true.

The following day I sold my old car, the *Singer* 9 HP, to Bobby Langdown who had the small garage opposite what was then the *Harmonic Hall* in Ashington. He gave me £200 for it. The car had done over 40,000 miles, and I got £10 more than I paid for it, so I was satisfied. Cars were scarce in '49. Bobby then did up the engine and sold the car at a profit.

I wasn't the only lucky lad in '49. Rusty's father, Jimmy, had bought a ten-shilling *Irish Sweepstake* ticket from a ticket seller at the Ashington pit, named Bill Robinson. It was for the Grand National, and Jimmy Mann was fortunate enough to draw a horse: *Royal Mount*. The news spread like wildfire in Ashington: "One of the lads at the pit has a horse in the Grand National Sweepstake." He was approached by a bookmaker from Glasgow to buy his ticket for £800. But Jimmy said "If I've been lucky enough to draw a horse, I'll stick with it."

Rusty's family were extremely excited and, on the day of the race, we all listened in to the BBC radio commentary. Jimmy's horse was second over the last fence to a horse called *Russian Hero* but was beaten into third place by *Riomond*. The result was: 1st Russian Hero; 2nd Riomond; 3rd Royal Mount. Jimmy had won £5000. In 1949, to a surface worker at Ashington Colliery, that was a fortune. It meant a whole new way of life for Jimmy and Ada, his wife, Colin, Wilf, Billy, Joyce Rusty, Ada, named after her mam, and Lily, the youngest girl.

Sadly, the youngest son, Freddie, had been killed in the Navy during the war. After two trips to Murmansk, in Russia, he had been on escort duty in the Atlantic approaches with his ship *The Curasoa*, a cruiser that had gone out to escort the *Queen Mary* on her way from America, loaded with American servicemen. They were on a zig-zag course. The *Queen Mary* ran straight over the cruiser, and Freddie, who had just gone on duty in the boiler room, was killed. There were only eight survivors, one of them was Freddie's mate, a Newbiggin lad called Joe Murray. Freddie was only 19 years old.

Colin, the oldest son, had been taken prisoner by the Germans on the island of Cos. He was then in the *Durham Light Infantry* who had been sent to the island to fight a holding action knowing they would either be taken prisoner or killed. The DLI were told they would not be taken off the island and to hold out as long as possible.

Billy was also in the Navy and had refused to be on the same ship as Freddie in the event of them both going down together. Billy was on the *Warspite* in the Med when she was bombed. The bomb went straight down the funnel of the ship and straight through the hold without exploding. He was on duty in the boiler room at the time and the noise burst both his eardrums. The ship managed to limp to Valletta harbour in Malta, but she was very low in the water. Her decks were awash, but she made it. Bill was in sick bay for months, but he fully recovered.

Wilf was a builder in the construction field and spent most of the war building and repairing airfields.

One Sunday afternoon the pub was closed and we had all just finished lunch. The back door bell rang. I went down to answer it, and there, standing at the door, was a chap from *St Mary's Motors*, Newcastle. He had come to enquire about a car that my brother-in-law Don Bailey had for sale, an *Austin* 16 HP. Don and my sister Dora were upstairs at the time. They had called to the *Portland* and stayed for lunch. I told the car dealer to wait and said I would tell Donnie to come down and see him.

The car dealer said "Whose car is that?" and pointed to my MG.

I told him it was mine, and that it was only a few weeks old.

He said "I'll give you £1200 cash for it now, as it stands."

I said, "I'm sorry, it's not for sale," and went upstairs to tell Donnie he was wanted.

Donnie came down to see to him and, as I sat down in the living room where my dad was having his afternoon nap, I mentioned that I had been offered £1200 for my car. You'd think someone had shot my dad: He sat bolt upright, realising what I had said. "Did you say £1200?"

I said "Yes, but I don't want to sell it.

"You must be wrong in your mind. Do you realise how much that is?"

He became very excited. "Bring the man up. Let's take the money."

My mother told him to calm down. "If Bill doesn't want to sell the car that's it. He's waited long enough for it and if he sold it he would have to wait another three years for another one."

So she settled the argument. It took my dad weeks to get over that.

Meanwhile, Rusty and I saw each other as often as we could and enjoyed the car and where it could take us, petrol rationing permitting. We liked going to the Newcastle *Empire Theatre* to see live variety shows. I remember going to see one of our favourites, Nellie Lucher, a coloured singer who played the piano with just drums and bass as back up. One of the songs was *He's Got Such a Fine Brown Frame*. Another was *My Mother's Eyes*. Rhythm was her middle name. She was great. That night, after the curtain came down and the lights went up, as we stood up to go, about four rows down from us in the stalls was my cousin Betty with her husband, Ronnie Hay. They were also great fans of Nellie Lucher. She was a star.

Jimmy James was another *must* for me, not so much for Rusty. Ronnie Ronalde, Ronnie Hylton and Max Bygraves. All great variety stars. You could see them all at the *Empire* for as little as four and a tanner in the stalls.

Rusty had never been to the Races at Gosforth Park so we decided to go to the June Meeting, '49, Newcastle's Race Week, the day before *Northumberland Plate*. Rusty wore a dark green satin dress and white court shoes. I was dressed in a sports jacket and grey flannels. It was a beautiful day, warm and sunny, until the second race, then the heavens opened up and it poured down for the rest of the afternoon. We were both drenched. Poor Rusty was soaked to the skin – not a winner – not a good day.

The highlight of the day was meeting my old school teacher Paddy Grimes, who had his daughter with him. Her first day at the Races too. We were all glad to get home and get dried out.

Learning the Bar Trade...at Hexham

That summer, Bill Norrie, the outside Manager for *McEwans* Breweries, asked if I would be willing to do some holiday relief work as it would give me some more experience in running a pub myself. He knew I had a car so the travelling was no problem. He asked if I could do two pubs in Hexham for him, the *Grey Bull* and the *Fox and Hounds*. I agreed. Bill said I would have to do two weeks at the *Grey Bull* first and follow on with two weeks at the *Fox and Hounds*. Kit Foxhall managed the *Grey Bull* with his wife Joan. I had met them when they had managed *The Widdrington Inn*. They knew me and were happy to have me as their relief manager. The *Grey Bull* was an average-sized country town pub: a bar and a buffet-cum-lounge, with an off-sales department just off the main bar and small cellar below the bar.

 Kit and Joan gave me the run of the house, showed me where everything was, then off they went on holiday. I had a part-time barmaid to help me and a morning cleaner. The procedure when you take over as holiday relief is: the stocktaker arrives about 9 am, checks the stock with you and the outgoing manager, who both sign to agree the stock. Then off he goes; off the manager goes; and you're on your own to get on with it.

 Now every barman all over the world is at a disadvantage with the customer unless he knows them as regulars. When a customer comes into the bar, he knows your status and who you are, but you don't know who or what he may be. You have to be able to recognize him immediately by his dress: what's he wearing? What's his accent? And his attitude? You have to work all this out by the time it takes to serve him with a drink. The barman also knows that the character of a customer can change completely after a few drinks, from a quiet character to a raving madman. Not an easy job.

 I had none of these problems at the *Grey Bull*. Tuesday is Market Day in Hexham, a busy day for the pubs with all the farmers coming into town. The 'bull walloppers' usually got a bit noisy after their day's work, but other than that it was a pleasant two weeks I spent there. I socialised with the regulars, and one of them invited me to see his cousin's pub, near Allendale, called the *Cart's Bog Inn*. His cousin made us most welcome. He was a great big man, about twenty stones in weight, but a gentle, quiet spoken man. He took me into his cellar – more like a farmhouse pantry – to sample his beer, which was drawn from the wood and standing on high gantries. The beer was in perfect condition and I told him so, which seemed to please him. We stayed and had tea, then back to the *Grey Bull* for opening time, 6 pm.

Mrs Foxhall's sister and her husband managed the *Fox and Hounds*. Ruth and Garth Hetherington. Garth came down to introduce himself and to offer any help if I needed it. After my two weeks at the *Grey Bull* I was going up to his pub for two weeks as his holiday relief. Garth was a Hexham lad, born and bred. His father had kept a butcher's shop in the west-end of Hexham all his working life, so Garth knew Hexham and the surrounding countryside well – a grand lad.

Kit Foxhall and his wife came back from holiday on the Sunday, and after taking stock on the Monday morning I was ready to go up and do the same thing at the *Fox and Hounds*. Before leaving, Kit pushed a fiver into my hand. I thanked him very much and went up to take over the *Fox* for two weeks.

While I was in Hexham, Rusty came up to see me whenever she was able, at weekends and an odd night through the week. She helped me behind the bar when I needed help, and we both enjoyed our time in Hexham.

Ruth and Garth were staying at home for the first week of their holidays. Ruth had just had a baby girl, a bonny little baby, with bright ginger hair, so they had decided to have only the second week away.

The *Fox* was more of a family pub with the public bar at the front and a well-kept lounge directly behind, with a passage to another small sitting room at the back, and the usual toilet facilities at the rear of the pub. Ruth and Garth had two barmaids who were sisters with a French-sounding surname; one of them was called Yvonne, a bonny blonde girl. Her sister had brown hair, a pretty petite little girl, both good workers.

The *Fox* also had a cricket team which played in the local league. They asked me if I would be willing to play for them in a Wednesday night game at Haydon Bridge. Wednesday nights were quiet, so I said I'd have a go. I hadn't played cricket since leaving school, but they were willing to give me a try. Haydon Bridge batted first, but we got them out for a reasonable score. Then we went in to bat. I was one of the tailenders and I remember the look on the faces of the Haydon Bridge lads after I had played my first stroke. They all moved in like a pack of vultures and I was out before the over ended. It was a memorable experience.

Garth was keen on golf and on the first week of his holidays he took full advantage of his time off to visit the Hexham golf course. He also liked trout fishing on the upper reaches of the Tyne from Hexham. He had arranged to go fishing one afternoon with two of his pals and he asked me if I would like to go along. I said I'd be delighted. His friends were brothers and they had a factory in Hexham that made all sorts of brushes. They were Jewish lads who had never been fishing before, but they were keen. Garth took us to some likely places on the river where we might get a catch, but the river was very low and slow-running. We'd had no rain for some time and the fish weren't biting. The tallest of the brothers was determined to get a bite and he ventured too far out on the slippery rocks in the river. He was wearing a beautifully-tailored suit and brown suede shoes. Suddenly he slipped and fell backwards into the river. Fortunately the river was shallow at that point and he was only soaked up to the waist. That finished our fishing expedition. The same lad is now fishing correspondent for the local paper, the *Hexham Courant.*

I spent a pleasant month in Hexham, at the best time of the year; long warm days and quiet sleepy nights, and made life-long friends of Ruth and Garth. Hexham holds some pleasant memories for me.

After my stint as relief manager, it was back to the old routine at the *Portland*, Ashington. Both Rusty and I were pleased to be back together; we could see each other every day now, and that meant a great deal to both of us.

Jimmy Mann had found it easy to be a Communist when he had nowt. But with his win of £5000 it had become that much more difficult. He had three sons and three daughters. Two sons married, one, Wilf, divorced and living at home; and three daughters, all courting strongly. After the initial flurry of parties and celebrations for his win, the pressure started to get to Jimmy. Now he seemed to have a lot more friends and relations than he thought he had. Jimmy still kept his Communist ideals, but he realised that he couldn't go on giving handouts to all his new-found friends and relations. He decided he would look around for a business. A newsagent's, preferably. In the meantime Rusty had sat and passed her senior Clerical Officer's exam for the civil service, but to qualify for promotion she had to spend two years in another department. This turned out to be His Majesty's Stationery Office, Keysign House, Oxford Street, London.

Rusty went to London in the October of '49, on her first night she stayed at a civil service hostel, but one night there was plenty. Fortunately, an old workmate of hers who had worked with Rusty in the Morpeth office, called to see her the following day at work. Her name was June Murray. June suggested that Rusty stayed with her, at her mother's London house, until they could find a flat to share. After a few days they found a flat in Tufnell Park, which they shared for the rest of Rusty's London stay. Rusty worked in the copyright department of HMSO. This entailed granting permission to magazines, newspapers etc, requesting the right to reprint or quote from Governmental Department Publications, eg Hansard, Agricultural Ministry etc. Interesting work, but not interesting enough for Rusty. She stuck it until May, then decided to come home and take another job until her dad was fixed up with his newsagent's business, which she was going to help him run. Rusty obtained a job as van driver for *Reyrolles* factory in Ashington, and stayed there until her dad bought his shop, in a small village in Durham called Hunwick. This meant that Rusty would be about fifty miles away from Ashington most of the week and we would only see each other twice a week. I went to Hunwick on my day off, and came back early the following morning. Rusty would come to Ashington on Saturday night and return on Sunday night.

She had to be up at 5 am each morning to drive her dad – he couldn't drive – down to Hunwick Railway Station to collect the newspapers from the early train; bring them back; sort them; and deliver them to customers in the village. After that she spent the rest of the day running the shop. A long day.

Learning the Bar Trade...at Winlaton

This was our way of life right until 1950. We seemed to spend most of our time driving to and from Ashington and Hunwick. In the summer of '50, Bill Norrie asked me if I would do another relief job for him, this time at the *Rose and Crown*, in a small village on the Tyne which had once been renowned for iron chain making, Winlaton. The locals called it the *Low Toon End* and it was managed by Enoch and Jessie Hughes: a couple of real characters. I had known them in Ashington when they were Steward and Stewardess of the *Grand Street* Club.

The *Rose and Crown* was then still lit by gas lamps; it had been an old coaching house. I took over on the Monday morning. After the stocktaking, Nocha introduced me to Mary the barmaid, a canny lass, auburn hair, bonny lass, and a little older than me. We worked well together. Before they left for their two week holiday, Nocha said "Come down to the cellar and I'll introduce you to Jimmy, my pet frog." We went down the cellar which had a low ceiling. We had to walk in a stooped position and Enoch called out for Jimmy the frog, and sure enough, Jimmy popped out from behind the barrels.

"I want you, Bill, to look after him while I'm away."

I said I would do just that.

"He doesn't eat much. Just a bit of lettuce now and again. He keeps the slugs down in the cellar."

"Oh, I see," I said.

It was a busy little pub, the *Rose and Crown*, Winlaton. The pit was still going then, just down the bank from the pub. And the regulars were mostly pitmen, so coming from Ashington I got on well with them.

Two things that I remember about Winlaton: the first Saturday night we had been busy. We employed an old man called Tommy who was potman and bottleman. At closing time he collected all the glasses, sorted the empty bottles, and carried them out into the bottle store in the old stables in the yard. A number of customers went out the back way, and old Tommy had given two brothers a case of bottled beer, the beer was called *Double Century McEwan's*. The brothers had quaffed a lot of booze and they carried the case of stolen beer home with them. The next morning the brothers came into the bar at opening time, Sunday 12 noon, carrying a metal beer case full of empty bottles. They said they had picked it up by mistake, last night, that they were sorry and they didn't want to get me into trouble with the breweries, and could they pay for them? I told them the bottles were one and a tanner each. They paid up and asked if it would be safe to stay and have a drink. I said "Yes, why not?" Now I know for a fact there are at least two honest men in Winlaton.

The other thing I remember is being invited to a day's fishing with the chap who lived next door to the pub, a fair-haired lad – married with one or two children. However, we decided to go up to Allenheads, where he said there was some good free trout fishing. We went in my MG car, and it didn't take us long to get there. The fishing was poor, for the first hour, until it started to rain, heavy rain, and the fish went mad, taking anything we cast at them. We both got soaked, but had a grand day's fishing.

Enoch and Jessie came back from holiday and I handed the pub over to them after stocktaking on the Monday morning. They thanked me, and off I went back to Ashington and home again.

Learning the Bar Trade...at Crook

Another unexpected job I was given in 1950 was to go to a place in Durham called Crook, to take over the management of the *Surtees Hotel* on the corner of the market square. This time I was asked by another outside manager for the breweries called Norman Wright. He was a quiet spoken gentleman who had been manager of the *Park Hotel*, Tynemouth. He asked me to meet him at the *Dun Cow* in Willington at 10 am on the Monday morning. From there I drove him to Crook in my car. He told me that the manager had been sacked and I was to take over until the breweries replaced him. When we arrived at the *Surtees* it was deserted except for an official stocktaker. We checked the stock together and I took over. There was no sign of the manager, and I was told he would be living upstairs for a few days until he could find other accommodation. I was not to allow him behind the bar under any circumstances.

Norman handed me the keys to the pub and then asked if I would be kind enough to give him a lift in my car back down to the *Dun Cow* in Willington where he had left his car. I took him from Crook to Willington in record time. He never forgot that car ride. I then returned to the *Surtees* and prepared to open up the pub.

About an hour later the manager returned. He had been called into the breweries office in Newcastle and given the sack, while we were taking over the pub, changing all the locks etc. This chap's name was Jack Stephenson and his nickname was *Plastic Jack*. The first thing he said to me as he walked in behind the bar was "I don't hold any of this against you son. I won't give you any trouble."

Just as he said this, a Great Dane came galloping into the bar. Jack said "It's alright, he won't bite."

He also had a parrot in a cage behind the bar, which he asked to leave until things were sorted out. I told him I was not supposed to let him come behind the bar on orders from the breweries.

He said "I won't take anything and I won't do you any harm, you can trust me, and bugger the breweries."

I said "OK then." There wasn't much else I could do under the circumstances, and I would only be there for a few weeks at most.

Learning the Bar Trade...at Crook

In that time I got to know Jack and his wife quite well. His wife was a bonny lass, quiet and reserved, completely different to Jack, who was larger than life, an outgoing personality, full of vitality, and always good for a laugh. I liked him. Jack had been an engineer in the Merchant Navy during the war, and on his trips to America he had learned how to make plastic. Being an engineer he found it easy to pick up the formula and mechanics of the thing. When the war ended he started up in a small way making plastic rain coats and handbags etc in North Shields. He went around the pubs and clubs there, selling the coats and bags until he built up a good business and opened a small factory to produce more merchandise.

In those days you had to give clothing coupons for raincoats and macks, but coupons weren't required for plastic coats. So Jack had a ready market for all the plastic coats he could produce. Soon after, he sold his factory and business for £24,000 and went with his wife on an extended holiday to South Africa. Being Jack, he spent most of the money enjoying life, safaris etc, until he was offered a job demonstrating agricultural machinery. His wife's health began to deteriorate, because of the climate, and Jack had to pack in his job and come home to England. And that's how he ended up in Crook, managing a pub for *McEwans* Breweries. And that's one of the reasons why he probably never hit it off with the underlings who helped to run the breweries – he didn't give a damn!

The last time I saw Jack he was acting as relief manager at the *Red Lion*, Bedlington. Good Luck Jack.

I learned a lot about life in those few short weeks at the *Surtees Hotel*, Crook. You never know what life has to dish out for you.

Late in 1950, Rusty and I decided to get married. We had been engaged for some time, and Rusty agreed to go in with me to manage a pub for the breweries. I asked my dad to approach Mr Norrie, the outside manager, to see if he could fix us up with a pub. Each time Norrie called at the *Portland*, my dad conveniently forgot to ask him about a pub for me – he didn't want me to leave the *Portland*. I was more or less running the pub for him, and it would mean depending on a stranger to help him run the *Portland*, which was a big pub.

However, after a number of convenient lapses of memory, I decided to ask Norrie myself about a pub. We wanted to be on our own.

Kell takes a Bride...and the *Crown and Anchor*, Low Walker

The next time Norrie came I approached him myself. That same day, he phoned me from his office in City Road, Newcastle, and asked if I could meet him there the following morning at 9 am. He had a pub for me but couldn't tell me where it was until the following morning. I said "OK, I'll be there."

I met him the following morning at the City Road office, and he told me the pub was called *The Crown and Anchor* in a place called Low Walker on Tyne. The manager had been dismissed on a minute's notice and I had to take over right away. Bill Norrie promised that if I decided to take the pub, the breweries would redecorate it throughout and have it ready in time for Rusty and I to move into as soon as we were married. I said "That sounds fair enough," and agreed to take it on the spot. The stock was taken and the pub was handed over to me that morning. This would be some time in April '51 and we were to be married on the 21st of June. In the meantime I had to travel each day between Ashington and Low Walker.

I had inherited one cleaner with the pub, but no other staff. So I asked for volunteers from the staff at the *Portland* to travel with me whenever necessary to help me run the *Crown and Anchor*. I got one volunteer from the staff at the *Portland*: Winnie Thompson, and the offer of help at the weekends from one of my pals, Eric Quinn. We carried on running the pub like this until Rusty and I were married.

Meanwhile, Dick Kitchen, who was Foreman Painter for the breweries, moved in with a squad of men to redecorate the whole of the pub, inside and out, and made a special effort to paper and paint the flat upstairs the way Rusty and I would like it. They were still at it when I left to be married. Dick said as I left "Don't worry, Bill, it will be all done by the time you get back from your honeymoon."

Rusty and I had decided to have a simple, quiet wedding. Rusty's two sisters had been married the previous year, and another big wedding wasn't a starter as far as we were concerned. Because of our fathers' opposing political views we had decided to have only two witnesses at our wedding and no family from either side – so there wouldn't be any argument as to who should be there and who shouldn't be there. We asked Jackie and Laura Milburn to be our best man and bridesmaid. Both of them accepted and were pleased to do the honours. Everything was arranged accordingly and was going beautifully until Jackie got word that he had been picked to play football for England against Spain that weekend. Panic stations! Who to ask to fill in for Jackie? Laura said she could still be bridesmaid and my pal Eric Quinn offered to replace Jackie as best man.

On Thursday, June 21st, 1951, the four of us set off for Morpeth Registry Office to be married at 11.00 am. The ceremony was conducted in a small room, up an alleyway, which is now the Bridge Street entrance to the Sanderson Arcade, not a very romantic setting, but by 11.30 am we were well and truly married. Back home to the *Portland* and a small welcoming party consisting of Nancy Robinson, her sister Jean, and Jean's daughter Joyce, forming an archway of cleaners' mops as we entered the back door of the *Portland*, on our way up to a champagne buffet that my mother had arranged. When it was over, we changed, thanked Laura and Eric, and sped off in the MG for a honeymoon in Brixton, Devon. Rusty had arranged the itinerary and our first night was spent at the *Chase Hotel* in York, which was managed by a nice couple who made us welcome.

The following day we set off for the *Northcliff Hotel* in Brixton. We arrived just in time for dinner, after a pleasant drive down through the West Country. The weather was warm and sunny and the only hitch was at Salisbury. We had stopped for a meal, and, as it was market day, the place was crowded and the narrow streets were no help, most of them being one-way only. After our meal, and on our way out of town, I managed to drive the open MG down a one-way street the wrong way. All the stall holders were shouting at me, pointing out that I was driving the wrong way. At the end of the street standing on point duty was a rather large policeman. I pulled up and apologised, saying I was a stranger to the area.

His reply was "Not another bloody Geordie." However, he managed to put us on the right road and we reached our destination without further mishap.

The *Northcliff* was a rather posh hotel at that time. The majority of the residents were in their fifties or sixties, all rather well off, so we were completely left on our own, which we didn't mind a bit.

The weather was kind to us in Devon, and with the open car we visited some beautiful and interesting places: Totnes, Paignton, Babbacome, Buckfastleigh Abbey, Princetown, up over Dartmoor. We regularly used the ferry across from Brixton to Torquay. Plenty to do and lots to see, a lovely place, Devon. During our second week I tried to teach Rusty how to swim in the open-air pool in Brixton, without much luck. All I got for my pains was a sunburnt back and shoulders, which was inconvenient, to say the least! Rusty still can't swim.

We had a run down to Dartmouth one day to watch the Naval College Cadets doing their thing in rowing boats and sailing dinghies – they are a breed on their own: pure thoroughbreds and born leaders, no wonder they call the Royal Navy the *Senior Service*.

We spent a night in Dartmouth at a pub with a thatched roof. They were selling scrumpy, a cloudy looking cider. Strangers were only allowed two glasses of scrumpy per head, and after two glasses you knew why. Dynamite!

Our two-week honeymoon was over all too soon and it was back to reality, back home to the North East, and moving into the *Crown and Anchor*, Low Walker, to start our career as publicans.

The *Crown and Anchor* was at the bottom-end of Fisher Street: a row of thirty terraced houses, one-up-one-down type, and at the top of Fisher Street was the *Ship Hotel*, a similar type of pub, owned by another brewery. Just one hundred and fifty yards down, towards the bottom of Welbeck Road, was the *Royal Hotel* the locals called the *Hobby*. Three pubs in a row of 300 yards! Plenty of competition, and another 100 yards either way was *The Victoria*, nicknamed the *Green Bar*, and the *Neptune Hotel* just outside the entrance to the Neptune Shipyard. Five pubs in 500 yards!

The painters had made a good job of the pub, and it looked bright and clean. The bar was long and narrow with the counter running the full length. A door at the top of the bar went out to the 'gents' and then out into a small back yard. There were three rooms which were served from a hatch at the back of the bar passage; one room that would seat about thirty and the other two were very small; they would seat about ten in each room. A pub typical of the area.

When we took over, the pub was taking between one and two hundred pounds a week, so we decided to have a go and build up the business. It had potential, and just needed a lot of hard work to get it running full steam. The *Anchor* had a football team playing in the Tyneside Sunday League. It also ran two darts teams; one male and one female; they both played in the local league, but needed reassurance that we would allow them to carry on running their teams as before which we gave with our wholehearted support. All that settled, we knuckled down to running the business.

Rusty and I were like two lambs who had been led by the *Judas* goat to the slaughter: inexperienced, eager-to-please, in the east-end of a bustling city. Coming from a small town like Ashington where everyone knew everyone else, it took some getting used to. But we soon learned how to survive.

In 1951, Wighams Richardson's yard was building a ship called the *Patricia*, a beautiful liner which was to be used to bring passengers from Scandinavia to see the Festival of London. It was to anchor in the Port of London and be used as a Hotel while its passengers visited the Festival. The *Patricia* was nearing completion when Rusty and I took over the *Crown and Anchor*, and I remember a lad called Butch Mather who was working as an electrician on the ship telling me "We'll never get that ship finished. The day-shift are fixing the electrical fittings in the bathrooms and the night-shift are stealing them."

However, they managed to finish her and she was ready to sail when one morning I had a visit by two local detectives from Hedlam Street Police Station. I had just opened the doors at 11 am when in walked these two large men wearing trilby hats and well-worn rain coats.

One of them was called Ken Scott. He said "Can we have a word?"

I said "Yes, what can I do for you?"

"Has anyone been trying to sell you a grand piano?"

I said "No, what would I want with a grand piano?"

Ken said "They've pinched a grand piano off the *Patricia* last night. It was only delivered yesterday."

An old man standing having a drink spoke up and said "I saw them slinging a piano over the side last night when I was on night shift, but I didn't take much notice." The piano was never recovered, and no more was heard about it.

All the shipyards on the Tyne were working to capacity in the Fifties, still replacing the huge tonnage that had been lost during the war. Jobs were easy to come by and men who were unemployed at that time, just didn't want work.

Each week the pub got busier, so we had to employ extra staff. Eric was still helping at weekends, but we needed a couple of good trustworthy barmaids to help out on weekdays so that Rusty and I could get a day off. We had a series of good lasses who came to work for us, but for one reason or another they had to leave either to get married, or because they were married and their husbands or their boyfriends objected.

Jackie Milburn Lends a Hand

I was talking to Jackie Milburn in Ashington about this problem one day and he said "I'll come and give you a hand on Tuesday and Thursday nights until you get someone, and you can have the loan of my England Caps and my Cup Winner's Medal to put on display behind the bar if you would like them."

When I mentioned this to the lads at the *Crown and Anchor* they couldn't believe it. 'Wor Jackie' was the pride of Tyneside and they couldn't dream that their hero would come to *their* pub to help out. They thought I was telling the tale, until the International Caps and his England and Newcastle shirts arrived, plus his FA Cup winner's medal. They made a stunning display behind the bar. The word spread from shipyard to shipyard up and down the Tyne, and people were coming from all over to see Jackie's caps and cup winner's medal.

The first night Jackie came to help out behind the bar was a Tuesday, usually not a busy night, but that evening the bar was packed solid, the rooms were packed solid, the passage was packed solid, and all there to see Jackie. They all wanted his autograph, so he didn't serve a lot of beer, but he certainly did some writing that night. Outside the pub, standing in a crowd, were about two hundred young kids waiting to get their idol's autograph. A police patrol car pulled up and two policemen came into the pub to see what was going on. When they saw Jackie behind the bar they simply asked him for his autograph and left.

The same thing happened whenever Jackie Milburn came down to Walker to help me out. And each night he came we took a week's takings in one night. Jackie wouldn't take a penny for helping me. Whenever anyone asked why he came he would say "Just tell them I'm your cousin, Bill." Every Saturday when United were playing at St James's Park, the bar would empty by 1.30 pm and all the lads would board the Trolley bus from the bottom of Welbeck Road, up to Gallowgate to see the match. After they had all gone I used to follow in the MG with a couple of ardent supporters, Shortie

Oswald and Tommy Smith. You *had* to go to the match on a Saturday or else you would be left out of the conversation in the pub for the rest of the week. The gates at St James's were usually around 60,000 at that time, and never any trouble, mainly because they were all Newcastle supporters. Few people travelled to away matches at that time in the '50s, they couldn't afford it. The only time we travelled was when Newcastle were having a run in the Cup, and in the early '50s that was so regular that most of the local supporters became financially embarrassed.

I remember in 1952 Newcastle made heavy work of their run in the Cup. They had replays at Sheffield, Leeds, and another at Portsmouth, which we all went to on a special train from Newcastle. The pitch at Fratton Park, Portsmouth was a quagmire and when Butlins Holiday Girls came out onto the pitch to give a dancing display before the match they were slipping and sliding all over the place. That match at Portsmouth was better than the Final as far as I was concerned. They were level at 2-2 near the end of the game and Portsmouth were pressing hard when Bobby Cowell, the Newcastle full back cleared the ball in desperation right up the field into the Portsmouth half where there was only Jackie and their centre half Jack Froggat standing. Jackie collected the ball by curving his leg around it then kicked it around and past Jack Froggat towards their goal. Jet Milburn gave Froggat about five or six yards start and passed him then crashed the ball into the back of the net. Every one of the Newcastle United fans went wild, even Field Marshal Montgomery who was a director at Portsmouth, was standing up and applauding. Before the commotion had died down, Newcastle had scored again through George Robledo, and that was it, the final result 4-2 to Newcastle. Wonderful!

A few days later I asked Jackie about that goal, I said "Why did you give Jack Froggat so much start for the ball, he could have fouled you?"

Jackie said "I knew he wouldn't, he doesn't play like that. I knew he would try to beat me fair and square, that's the way he plays."

John Beaton, one of my regulars, told me his brother was in the Navy stationed at Portsmouth and that the Navy lads were finding it difficult to get tickets for the Portsmouth game. I told him I would ask Jackie if he could get us some spare tickets to take down with us. Jackie got us six extra tickets which we took down. John had told his brother that we would be bringing six tickets with us and he was waiting for us at Portsmouth station with five of his Navy pals, when we arrived for the match. When we gave them the tickets the Navy lads were over the moon. They were pressing twenty packets of Navy-issue cigarettes onto us from all angles. They were so pleased, and saw the best game of the Cup run. We came home to Newcastle on the Sunday morning, a jubilant, but totally tired bunch of supporters, to wait for the build up to the Cup Final which was to be Arsenal versus Newcastle in 1952.

While I was away on these football excursions with the lads, Rusty and the staff looked after the pub. We had some grand lasses working for us: three full time barmaids; Marie, Emma and Nellie, all good workers who knew how to handle the customers. We had part-time staff we could call on for special occasions: Sally, Connie and Albert Embleton, a general dogsbody barman, concert chairman etc, he was on the dole yet had *three* jobs. Albert was up at 4.00 am to go to the Green Market to buy fruit and veg for greengrocers who didn't want to get up so early; then he'd go home, have an hour's sleep, and in the afternoon he worked part-time driving the hearse for the undertaker. In the evening he would be down at the *Crown and Anchor*, working for me if I needed him. And he was unemployed! He had also been a boxer at St James's Hall when he was younger: a three-rounder on the bill, to fill in the programme. Albert told me he used to get seven and sixpence for three rounds, and a dammed good hiding for his pains. He could also dish it out, and when he worked for me he was still a handy lad with his fists, if needs be.

We also had a cleaner, Pat Airs, who came in early morning to clean up the pub. A quiet girl who was married and lived just a few doors away from the pub. We were a good team. Albert's wife, Sadie also helped out whenever required.

We had a football team, a darts team and a ladies' darts team. They were all locals. The football team were mostly shipyard lads, all canny players. Curly Wilson was Captain and he would pick from a number of players whose names were, Bob Mulroy, Kenny Holmes, John Dobson, Jackie Burke, John Kelly, Joe Alcock, goalie, Michael Morrissey, Doug Hunter, Bob Hunter, Jimmy Christie, Peter Belshore, Joe Mulroy, Tommy Waugh, Bob Patterson, John Waite, Arthur Alexander and Alfie Whipp, all very keen lads. They always had good support from the rest of the regulars: Jimmy Fairbairn, George Matthews, Albert Embleton,

Jimmy Embleton, Joe Bradley, Tommy Smith and Shorty Oswald. The bus was jam packed when the team were playing an away game. They used to like playing the *Fellinggate Club*. The club always made them welcome after the game, for a drink and a sing song, and we did the same for them when they came to play us. The *Crown and Anchor* had their own team song, which they all sung with gusto whenever the occasion arose. It went like this:—

> *Give honour, give honour, to the Anchor lads*
> *Give honour, give honour, where it's due*
> *Don't forget the Anchor lads*
> *Are willing to play the game for you*
> *When they get upon the football field*
> *Some of them are mortal drunk*
> *But they play like devils*
> *To win the Cup and medals*
> *So give honour, give honour, where it's due.*

The money to finance the football team was raised by selling domino cards, at sixpence a try. It brought in fourteen shillings. Ten shillings was paid to the winning number, and four shillings into the football fund. This money paid for bus travel to away matches, football strips, rent and rates for our football pitch, which had been the wartime Ack Ack site in Low Walker, now just a piece of waste ground which we had to clear of an assortment of bricks, tin cans and dog droppings each Sunday morning we had a home match. The goal posts were permanently fixed, but we had to hang the goal nets each time we played, and take them down when we finished. This was all done by volunteers from the supporters of the team. The lads used the small back room of the pub as their changing room, and when they all had their football strips on, they would walk from the pub up to the pitch, which was about six hundred yards away.

One Sunday morning, Curly Wilson approached me, and said that the lads had asked him, to ask me, if it would be possible to have their photographs taken in their football strips with each one of them wearing one of Jackie Milburn's England caps, which I had on display in the bar. I said "I'm sure Jackie wouldn't mind." I had twelve caps on display at the time, so they each wore one with one left over for Shorty Oswald to wear. Shorty also put on Jackie's

Jackie Milburn Lends a Hand

black and white shirt and pants, and I took the photograph of them all sitting, and standing, as proud as peacocks. Shorty sat holding the football with *Crown and Anchor 1951* chalked on it.

The issue of the Cup Final tickets came around for the 1952 Arsenal versus Newcastle game at Wembley. The demand however, outstripped the supply. But Jackie managed to get a ticket for me, and a dozen three and sixpenny tickets for the lads in the bar. We decided the fairest way to allocate them would be a raffle with only regulars able to buy tickets. This was agreed and we decided to have the draw on the weekend before the game. In the meantime I had the Cup Final tickets pinned to the wall behind the bar, on display, just to let the customers see what they looked like.

A few days before we were due to raffle the tickets I had a mysterious 'phone call from a man with a haughty and arrogant voice. He said "I hear you have some Cup Final tickets for sale down there, brother. I'm sending some of my boys down today and you *will* sell them the tickets."

I said "Who the hell are you? The tickets are not for sale, and you needn't send your boys down here, brother." I put the 'phone down and forgot about it.

Later that morning Albert Embleton came into the bar: my first customer. He asked for a beer, then went over to practice on the dart board. I told him about the 'phone call and he said "It must be some crackpot from the town."

Twenty minutes later four rough-looking men walked into the bar and asked for four halves of best bitter. I served them and as I turned towards the till to ring in the cash, Albert was making all sorts of peculiar signs to me. I walked up the bar and asked him what was wrong. He replied "They're what's wrong. That's the heavy mob from the Bigg Market in the town."

I put two and two together, and the 'phone call started to make sense. There were four of them and only two of us, and Albert was frightened. So I took the bull by the horns and went up to talk to the four men. "What brings you down this neck of the woods then?"

The smallest one, thick set with a broken nose, said "Oh, just a run out, hinny."

It was then I recognised him. "Aren't you Billy Wood from Gateshead?"

He looked shocked. "Yes."

"You used to play darts for my dad, at The *Gloucester Inn*. My name is Bill Kell."

"Are you Billy Kell's son?" I nodded my head. He turned to the other three and said "Nark it. It's all off. Look, Bill, we've been sent down here to pinch those Cup tickets you've got pinned on the wall. Now take my advice and put them in a safe place."

I asked him how they were going to pinch the tickets. He said "Simple. We were to start a fight and when you came around to sort it out, one of us was going to jump over the bar and take all the tickets and just walk out while you were busy with the others."

They drank off and left. I never saw them again. I took Billy's advice and took down the tickets immediately. Albert was relieved when they went. "You're a lucky lad, Kell. Fancy knowing one of them."

That weekend we raffled the Cup tickets. The winners were delighted, but one or two of the lads were bitterly disappointed. I still managed to get them tickets but I had to pay the going rate, which was three pounds ten shillings for a three and sixpenny ticket. The lads were delighted and paid the money without a quibble.

We all left the Central Station on a Football Special train which took us straight to Wembley station. We walked up to the stadium, saw the match, a disappointing game, little excitement, poor football, Newcastle won 1-0. We walked back to Wembley station, back on the train, and home. We began to cheer up as we got nearer home, after all we'd won the FA Cup. Back in Newcastle, everyone was smiling, and laughing. We'd won the Cup. Once more they were all excited and delighted, so we joined in the celebrations. All the Geordies were in a good fettle. Winning the FA Cup certainly does something for a place and the city of Newcastle was no exception. Everyone was proud of the team, and the fact that Wor Jackie came down to help out occasionally at the *Crown and Anchor* made our regulars feel something special. They were proud and let everyone working on the Tyne know that Jackie Milburn was one of *us*.

The football euphoria lasted throughout the summer and Jackie promised that when the heat had died down and it was his turn to have the FA Cup to show to his friends etc, he would bring it down one night to let the lads see it close up, and make a special night of it. When I told the regulars they were thrilled, and a few weeks

Jackie Milburn Lends a Hand

later everything was arranged. We picked a Wednesday night because the shipyard lads were working an extra half shift on Tuesdays and Thursdays. The Wednesday would give them time to get home from work, get changed into their best suits, and down to the *Crown and Anchor* to welcome 'Wor Jackie' and the FA Cup.

We had all the staff working that night: Marie, Emma, Nellie, Albert and Sadie, Sally, Connie, and Eric came through from Ashington to help out. Jackie duly arrived with the local reporter from the *Ashington Post* and a photographer, and a large wooden box which held the famous FA Cup.

The place was crammed and everyone wanted their photograph taken with Jackie and the Cup. The photographer was kept busy for most of the night. The lad who took the bets in the shipyard – his name was Jimmy Ranson, had brought his boss down to the pub for the occasion. His boss's name was Mac McDougall and he asked me to fill the Cup with whisky and he would pay for it. I filled it with whisky, – four bottles – and the lads all had a sup out of it. Jackie had to leave early but he left the silverware with the reporter who was going to take it back to Ashington after we closed. We had a great night and, after closing time, all the customers had left, except the reporter and photographer plus Jimmy and Mac, Shorty Oswald and Tommy Smith standing talking in the bar. There was still a drop of whisky left in the Cup, and, with all the excitement of the night I had forgotten to lock the front door. It was now 10.45 pm. There was a noise in the front entrance of the pub, and the bar door slowly opened and in walked a great big ginger-haired policeman. He saw the FA Cup on the counter and it was written all over his face that we had stolen it. The *Ashington Post* man convinced him otherwise, and after he was assured it was all above board he took off his helmet and asked if he could have a drink out of the Cup. I said "By all means." What a relief.

The pub was popular and Friday and Saturday nights were always chaotic. On these nights a variety of Artistes or Buskers called in to ask if they could do a turn, play the accordion, sing a song etc. One man asked if he could show his paintings; he would hold the paintings above his head so that everyone could see them, showing about a dozen, portraits, landscapes etc, then he would go around with the hat for a collection. One little old, round-shouldered, grey haired man was a regular turn; he came in and asked me if he could bring his two lions in, to do a turn. He was dressed in a red waistcoat, top hat, black bow tie, taily coat and wellies with the tops turned down. He asked permission to use two wooden bar stools to set up his show at the top end of the bar. He carried a large whip in his right hand which he used in the act. When the stools were set up and everyone was informed that the act was about to begin, he would go out and lead in these two ferocious imaginary lions, and set about making them jump on and off the two stools. One lion was called Leo and the other Caesar. He always had a lot of trouble with Leo and it took a great deal of persuasion and whip cracking to get the lion to do as he was told. On a number of occasions Leo nearly had him, but he always managed to struggle free. The old man worked hard, and was always sweating heavily when he finished his act, after which he would go round with the hat. I was short of copper for change one night and asked him if he had any copper to spare. He emptied his pockets and I counted out thirty shillings worth; he said "That's all I've made tonight." It would be about 8.30 in the evening, and he could probably do another six pubs before the end of the night, so I reckoned he had a good thing going for him, all tax free, with only the two *imaginary* lions to feed.

The locals enjoyed the turns; there was always a bit of good humoured leg-pulling and banter, but they were always generous when the hat came round. We used to get a tall, dark, soft spoken man in at weekends selling mussels and whelks. He came up from North Shields with a basket over his arm. He sold the shellfish at sixpence per packet. One night I asked him if he could get me a lobster. He said "I'll bring you one next week. A nice one." Sure enough, the following Friday night in he came, smiling all over his face, "I've got you one, boss." And there, on top of his basket, was a large lobster with 7/6 marked in biro on the back of it. I went to get the money out of the till, and he turned to serve someone with a bag of mussels, and when we turned round, the lobster was missing from the top of his basket. It was a large lobster and difficult to hide. I was stunned. I stopped the barmaids from serving and told everyone in the bar that it was *my* lobster that had gone missing and there would be no more drink served until it was returned. There was a few seconds' silence and then pandemonium. No one had touched the lobster. No one had seen the lobster. I must be mistaken. It wasn't any of them. They wouldn't do a thing like that to me. However, the lobster had completely disappeared and I had to accept it. I paid the man for his lobster, shrugged my shoulders and told the barmaids to carry on serving.

The sequel to that fishy tale came twenty years later, at the *Junction Inn*, Widdrington. Rusty and I had a visit from one of our old ladies' darts team customers from the *Crown and Anchor*. Her name was Alice Anderson, by then seventy years old. She had asked her oldest son who was on leave from the Merchant Navy to hire a car and drive her out from Walker to Widdrington to confess to Rusty and I that it was *her* who had the lobster that went missing all those years ago. She said "Mind you, I didn't pinch it. It was passed along the bar and eventually pushed into my bag. And I was frightened to own up that I had it in front of everybody. I haven't got long to go now and it has been worrying me for a long time and I wanted to clear my conscience, before I go." Rusty could see she was upset and told her not to worry her head about a lobster and gave her a large drink. They started to talk about old times, after which she and her son left to drive home to Walker with Alice clutching a bottle of champagne that Rusty had given her.

We had no music and singing licence at the *Crown and Anchor*, only a mechanical music licence which covered playing the radio and the radiogram, so we had '78' records playing most of the time. The music could also be heard in the room through a speaker wired up to the radiogram. Occasionally we had an accordion player on a Saturday night for a real old-fashioned singsong. As this was against the law, we had a look-out posted at the front door. Alfie Meakle usually got this job. The locals called him *Blind Alfie*. He had poor sight, but he could smell a policeman a mile off. We were only caught out once, by a smart Police Sergeant. Alfie had seen him and a constable coming and rushed in to warn us. So everything was quiet when the sergeant and the constable came in to have a look around. They both gave me a nod as they left. Two minutes later *Blind Alfie* came in and said "It's OK, they've gone," and the music and singing started up again with a swing. It was going full blast when in walked the sergeant and constable; they had decided to double back to see what was going on. We were caught red handed. I was called to one side, in the passage, and given a severe telling off and told if it happened again I would be pinched. I said I was sorry and it would never happen again, and off they went. *Blind Alfie* got a right bollicking that night from everybody for letting us down, and was told to keep his eyes open in the future.

The ladies' darts team played on Tuesday nights, one at home, and one away. The home matches were popular with the regulars and were always well supported. The captain of the team was Mary Dandy, an extrovert lady who smoked cigarettes in a long holder, always good for a joke and a bit of leg pulling from the lads. She had a good team of lasses. They were: Nellie Beaton, Kitty Doyle, Kitty Dummigan, Marion Beaton, Alice Anderson, Annie Barr and Sadie Embleton. They also had a number of good supporters: Belle McGreavy, Renee Parkins, Jenny Airs, Edie Callabuton and many others whose names I can't recall.

On home games, each one of the players brought a large parcel of sandwiches to be handed out to everyone after the match was over. And it always ended with a sing song from the girls, very good singers, always entertaining, and it was good for business. They won the Darts League Cup in 1952 and it was presented to them at a big darts 'Do' at the Heaton Assembly Rooms. Mary Dandy was thrilled when she and the team went up on the stage to be presented with the Cup. There were hundreds of people there representing teams from the league which covered Byker, Walker, Heaton and Wallsend.

After the presentation the girls decided they would have their own special 'Cup Night' at the *Crown and Anchor*, with a nice buffet supper and a sing song for their supporters. They asked Jackie Harvey, whose father Matty, had the small general dealer's shop in the middle of Fisher Street, if he would make them a microphone to sing through. Jackie was clever at that sort of thing and he made them a mike from one of the earphones of an RAF pilot's helmet and wired it up to the radiogram and then to the speaker in the Room. It worked perfectly and was easy to hide if the police walked in. The microphone was the highlight of the evening. All the girls wanted a go at singing into the mike, and Albert, who was acting as Concert Chairman, had a job keeping them in order. I filled the Cup with whisky; it held one bottle. The girls all had a drink and then had their photographs taken with the Cup. They were all quite proud of themselves, and they all had a grand night.

Monday night was quiet, and if there was boxing on at St James's

Hall I would go up to see the fights. Teddy Gardener was at the peak of his career in the early '50s and I saw all of his fights at St James's. I was there the night he won the *Lonsdale Belt* and I recall Jimmy Wilde, The Welsh Wizard, being introduced in the ring that night before Teddy's fight. Teddy Gardener was a great favourite with the Tynesiders; he was a local lad from County Durham and St James's Hall was always a FULL HOUSE when he was on the bill. Another lad who was a Geordie favourite came from St Helens in Lancashire, his name was Wilf Glynn, a knockout specialist and if he hit them with his favourite punch they went down and stayed down. He did this for some months, until one night he was billed to fight a lad from Scotland. The Scotsman couldn't make it and the promoters brought in a substitute from London, a coloured lad called Yolande Pompey. Early in the fight Wilf caught the coloured lad with his Sunday punch and Yolande went down. Wilf walked to a neutral corner thinking it was all over, but after a short count Yolande got up and carried on boxing. One or two rounds later Yolande caught Wilf with an uppercut and Wilf went down. He staggered up but had lost all interest in the fight. I never saw Wilf Glynn box again at St James's Hall. Yolande Pompey went on to become a leading contender in the fight game.

The North East produced some good boxers between the wars. Men like Jimmy Falcus, Mickey McGuire, George Willis, John 'Boy' Page, Andy McLoughlin, Harry Lister; all tough hard men at their own weight.

Not long after I took over the *Crown and Anchor* I had a visit one morning just after opening time. In walked this dapper little man, smartly dressed in white shirt and silk tie, black jacket and pin striped trousers. He said "Hello, Bill, I'm John 'Boy' Page, an old pal of your dad's. I've got the *Queen's Head* in Byker. I've just called in to see how you're getting on, and to let you know if you need any help, or if anyone gives you any trouble, just let me know and I'll sort them out for you. I know most of the Bad Lads around here."

I said "Thank you very much, John. That's very kind of you." We became good friends, the time I spent in Walker. He took me under his wing and I was grateful for his kindness. George Willis was another good friend; he was working as a drayman for *McEwans* at that time and he did me one or two great favours when I was at the *Crown and Anchor*. He was another old friend of my father. Handy lads to have on your side in a tough neighbourhood.

Andy McLoughlin was an Ashington lad, and Harry Lister came from Lynemouth. I knew them both well, both hard, but canny lads.

A good number of boxers went in for a pub after their careers in the ring were over. Teddy Gardener took a pub in Durham.

One ex-boxer took a pub on Scotswood Road. He was keen on keeping fit and prided himself on his agility. One quiet afternoon he was sitting playing dominoes with a couple of his customers when an old deaf man came in, carrying a walking stick. As there was no one behind the bar the old man knocked on the counter with his stick. Now in those days the best beer was drawn from the wood in the cellar, and the ordinary beer was drawn up through the pumps on the bar counter. As the old man knocked on the counter the manager said to him "I'll be there in a minute, hinny."

The old man, being deaf, didn't hear him and began to knock on the counter for the second time. The manager clashed the dominoes down on the board, turned around, and with one hand, vaulted over the bar, forgetting he had left the cellar hatch open, as he disappeared down the cellar the old man reached over the bar and shouted, "I don't want Best, I just want Ordinary, hinny."

Nothing succeeds like success, and the *Crown and Anchor* was going very well. Mr Norrie was happy with the increase in the business and told me he had another job for me, if I was interested. He said that the breweries were starting an outside catering branch in conjunction with 'Parkers the Caterers' of South Shields. Parkers would be doing the food and I would be in charge of the drinks side of the business. I would have to provide the staff for the bars and organise the transport of the staff. It would entail a lot of travelling and would cover the whole of the North East. I said I was interested. Rusty and I talked it over and decided to have a go. Rusty was willing to look after the pub while I was away on the functions. The staff were all keen to help; they enjoyed the change of venue. We started off in a small way, one or two functions a week. I was paid £5 per function and the staff were on an hourly rate which was extra to their wage at the *Crown and Anchor*.

It was hard work but we all enjoyed it. We did functions at Stockton Town Hall; Londonderry Hall, South Shields; Durham College; Newcastle Dental College; Sedgefield Races; and Flower Shows and Agricultural Shows. It was all good experience and taught me how to organise staff and provide service to customers. If we were short of staff for a big function we always had plenty of volunteers from the lads in the bar: Shorty Oswald, Bob Alcock, Curly Wilson and his wife, Ronnie Parkins, Albert Embleton and a dark-haired lad called Frank. They all worked as a team and were a great help to me. The outside catering carried on right up until we left the *Crown and Anchor*. Good times.

About this time I had a visit from a chap called George Stewart, who was looking for pub sites to place table football machines which he said had just been imported from Belgium. I said I'd be interested, so he arranged to have a machine delivered. The football table was a great success and within weeks most pubs in our area had a table, enough of them to form a Football Table League. The first year of the League the *Crown and Anchor* won hands down. Rusty and I won the pairs cup that year at the *Station Hotel* Killingworth. George Stewart presented us with the cup and £25, which made for a good night. The Football Table game proved popular for many years after. In that year, 1952, we also had a couple of our lads in the men's pairs final. Bob Alcock and Bill Smith represented the *Crown and Anchor*, and the Final was played at the *Olde Cross Inn*, Ryton on Tyne. We all went up to give the lads our support, and they didn't let us down. They won the Football Table Final, and each received a Cup which we had inscribed with their names. And we got Jackie Milburn to come down to present them with the cups a week later. Bob Alcock and Bill Smith had their photographs taken with Jackie Milburn receiving the cups. It was an extra special night for those two lads. They were proud of their achievement.

One quiet Monday night there were only a few customers in the bar, Jackie Carruthers, one of the football team lads, Tommy Waugh and John Beaton were in playing darts, when one of them suggested a bus trip down to Wallsend to have a look around one or two pubs for a change of scene. As it was quiet in the bar I decided to join them, and off we went by trolley bus to Wallsend. Our first port of call was the *Coach and Horses*. It was busy; they had a concert party on and the whole pub was full. We tried one or two more pubs, *The Robin Hood*, *The Victoria*, and the *Penny Wet* and eventually ended up back at the *Coach and Horses* to round off the evening. At closing time we left to get the trolley bus home and called into the fish and chip shop on the way. I was standing at the counter of the shop as a lad in front of me got served and was putting salt and vinegar on his chips when a little perfectly-shaped grey-brown hand came out from the inside of his jacket and picked up a chip and went back inside his jacket. I was intrigued by this mysterious little hand and asked, "What's that you've got?"

The lad said "It's a grass monkey." He partially opened his jacket and there, snuggled in and clinging on to his shirt, was a monkey that looked most forlorn and tired. It had a small dog's collar around its waist with a fine chain attached to it. The lad said "It's for sale if you're interested. I'm going into the RAF soon and my mother says I've got to get rid of him before I go."

I said "How much do you want for him?" He said "Seven pounds," and there in the light of the fish and chip shop window we started to haggle over the price. I told him I only had £4.10.0 with me and offered him that. He said "OK then, but promise you'll look after him." I said I would. "He eats almost anything, fruit, nuts, bread, biscuits, and if he gets naughty just smack his bum," he said.

I collected the monkey, put him in my jacket and went to get the trolley bus home. We got on the bus at Station Road, on to White Street, past the pawnshop and down past *Simpson's Hotel* and on home to Walker. When I walked in with the monkey Rusty was taken aback, at first. I think 'shocked' would be a better word. She said "What are we going to do with him?"

I said "It's late, we'll just have to put him in a cardboard box on a blanket for tonight, and I'll sort him out in the morning." We put him in a box and placed the box in the bottle store at the end of the bar. I then shut the door so he wouldn't get out.

The following morning Rusty was up early and went down to see how Jacko the monkey was doing. She came back up and walked into the bedroom, saying "You'd better go down and see to your friend, he's causing chaos in the bottle store, and he's got the cleaner terrified."

Suffering from a slight hangover, it wasn't the sort of news I wanted to hear, but I got up, quickly dressed, and went down to see what Jacko was up to. When I opened the bottle store door he was sitting on top of a stack of metal beer cases filled with empty *Export Ale* bottles. He was picking the bottles out, one by one, putting them to his mouth, and with his right foot he was tipping the bottles up and drinking the dregs of beer that were left in the bottles. As he was emptying them he was dropping the bottles with a crash onto the concrete floor. When he saw me he started bouncing up and down in the same position, on top of the beer case, monkey fashion and banging on his chest with his hands, like King Kong, trying to scare me. I called his bluff and walked over to him. I grabbed him with my left hand and he immediately sank his teeth into my thumb. My reaction was to clout him hard with my right hand. This had two immediate results: it sobered him up and he started to wimper and cower like a frightened child. I picked him up and he cuddled into me, begging for comfort. Jacko was subdued for the rest of the day. Rusty took him from me and nursed him like a baby saying to me "You big bully, you didn't have to hit him like that."

I said "I'm sorry," and from that morning Jacko took over our lives. He instinctively knew when anyone was afraid of him, and always took full advantage of them. Two of the barmaids were scared to death of him, Emma and Nellie. Marie was much older and it would take more than a small grass monkey to frighten her. The first thing we had to do was get him a secure cage. One of the lads, Bob Wilson, volunteered to make him a cage. Bob was a shipwright in the shipyard, and within a couple of days Jacko was fixed up with a beautifully-made cage which we kept behind the bar. Jacko liked his cage to retreat to, or to hide in, but he also loved to be out and about. He loved to show off in front of the customers and on a cold morning we would let him out to sit in front of the fire warming his hands just like a little old man.

If he got half a chance he would jump up and pull Emma's hair. She used to let out such a scream, while he ran and hid in his cage. Emma could express herself for a Walker lass, and some of the things she said about the monkey were not for a vicar's ears. "That bloody monkey, I'll wring his bloody neck," was one of her more acceptable expressions. All the lads in the bar thoroughly enjoyed it when Emma got herself worked up. They egged her on to do all sorts of things to the monkey. Some of the banter was hilarious and Emma was always good for a laugh.

When any foreign seamen came into the bar Jacko was always the centre of attraction. Many of them couldn't speak English, but Jacko understood them and was always pally with them. One day a bunch of Norwegian seamen came in and Jacko picked an expensive fountain pen out of the top pocket of one of them and promptly began to eat it. The monkey was covered in ink in no time and the seamen thought it a great joke. Another time one of the seamen was playing with him and Jacko picked two folded five pound notes out of his top pocket and ate them with great relish. The seaman just shrugged his shoulders and smiled. When it was fine and warm we used to let Jacko out into the yard on a long lead so he could sit on top of the yard wall and sun himself as he watched the world go by. The gents' toilet was out in the yard and Jacko's lead was just long enough to allow him to sit on top of the wall, leading into the urinals. One afternoon a man who had just been out to the gents' came back into the bar as white as a ghost and said "Give me a glass of whisky quick. I must be seeing things. I thought I'd seen a monkey sitting on the wall in the gents'."

After he drank the whisky I said "You're alright, you're not seeing things, it is a monkey and he belongs here."

The local kids soon got to know there was a monkey at the *Crown and Anchor* and when he was out in the yard some of them would open the back yard gate to get a better view. This meant they were within his range, and that could mean trouble, especially for the younger kids. They would get excited at seeing Jacko and this didn't always please him, causing him to bite a lot of the smaller children on the legs and hands. One day he took a small toy from one of the kids. It was a small plastic ball half filled with water, with a tiny plastic duck floating inside. It didn't take Jacko long to smash open the plastic ball and extract the small plastic duck. He played with that duck for weeks, and each time he finished playing with it he would put it into one of the food pouches that grass monkeys have on the side of their necks, just underneath their jaws. As he walked about you could see the outline shape of this plastic duck just under the skin of his jaw, and when he wanted to play with it he would just push it up the pouch and out of his mouth. That summer there was a steady stream of kids and seamen going up to Walker Road Hospital for injections against monkey bites.

One night we had a visit from Old Bob Hart and a friend of his, a young blond-haired lad who was in the Merchant Navy. They were both from Ashington and had come down to Walker for a night out. When the lad saw we had a monkey, he said "Does he like a drink?"

I said "He likes a whisky and peppermint."

The young lad said "Get him one in," and Jacko joined the company. He behaved himself well until he'd had his fourth whisky and peppermint. Then he started to act himself. He was as drunk as a 'Lord'. He had been sitting on the end of the counter and after his fourth drink he began jumping up and down and banging his chest. He was cracking anybody out to fight in his way. After about five minutes of this he fell off the counter, palatic drunk, and I had to put him into his cage to sleep it off. The next morning he was a sorry sight, sitting crouched in his cage, holding his head in his hands, and he could hardly open his eyes. Poor little mite. Rusty made him a cup of very sweet tea and crushed an *Aspro* tablet into it. That seemed to perk him up a bit, but he was ill all day. After that we kept him off the hard stuff. He was allowed a small glass of beer occasionally. Rusty and I took him with us in the car on our days off, he enjoyed riding in the car with the hood down. He liked riding on the luggage rack, on the back of the MG, when it was warm enough for him. Jacko made a comical sight, sitting on the back of the car, eating a packet of crisps, or licking an ice cream cornet and chattering at cars as they went past, with an astonished look on the drivers' faces.

After we closed at night and everything was cleaned away, and the staff had gone home, Rusty would let Jacko out of his cage for what she called his mad half hour. The monkey used to thoroughly enjoy himself, galloping up and down the bar, swinging hand over hand along the counter rail, then up the curtains and finally sitting on top of the curtain pelmet, then down again and along the bar at great speed. Occasionally we would get a knock on the bar window. Most of the pub managers knew what that knock meant in the Walker area. It was usually a couple of local bobbies wanting a pint on the house. I'm afraid Jacko soon put a stop to that. He was no respecter of the law, or the uniform. If they came in when he was having his mad half hour, he would try to pull off their lapel numbers, their tunic buttons, steal their helmets, and knock over their free pints. We never had any more window knocks after they found out that Jacko would be loose.

In his quieter, more relaxed moods, Jacko liked to sit and examine your hair. He would go through your hair thoroughly and examine every folical. It was his way of showing that he trusted you; he could be very lovable at times. At these moments he looked like a wise old man. One afternoon in the late summer of '53 I had a visit from one of the young policemen from Hedlam Street Station. He came into the bar and asked "Do you have a monkey?"

I said "Yes."

"The Inspector has sent me down to tell you to get rid of him. We have had a number of compaints from irate mothers about him biting their kids. And the last straw was a complaint from the Walker Hospital: they're running out of serum. They've been giving so many injections to people with monkey bites. You've got to get rid of him as soon as possible. That's my message from the Inspector. I don't care how you do it. You can put him in a bag and throw him in the Tyne, as long as you don't keep him in this area."

Rusty and I were both upset at the news, and were at our wits end to know what to do for the best. We couldn't ignore the police, yet we were loathe to part with Jacko. That night a friend from Whitley Bay called in to see us; his name was Rusty Miller who had a ladies' hairdressers in Whitley Bay called *Maison Miller*. When he heard the news about the monkey he immediately offered to take him. Mr Miller had visions of going around his hairdressing shop with the monkey on his shoulder, attending to his lady customers. He took Jacko home with him to Whitley Bay. After one night in his mother's house Mr Rusty Miller got an ultimatum. Jacko had smashed the house up during the night. "That monkey goes, or you both go."

That same day, Jacko was passed on to a Danish gentleman who was working as steward of the Royal Northumberland Yacht Club. The Dane, who was living ashore in Blyth, took Jacko as a pet for his two children. Rusty Miller had met him while visiting the Yacht Club as a social member, and had become friendly with him because Rusty was very proud of having Danish blood in his veins. Jacko's stay with the Danish family didn't last long. He bit both of the children and was passed on again, I believe to another publican. Both Rusty and I wished we had never parted with the monkey, but in our efforts to try and get him back we drew a blank. By the time we retraced Jacko's movements the Dane had left Blyth and we were unable to find out where Jacko ended up. I would like to thank Rusty Miller and Mr Cyril Kling, the Hon. Secretary of the Royal Northumberland Yacht Club for their help in trying to retrace the movements of our notorious little monkey. It was rumoured that Jacko had gone down with the ship when the headquarters of the Blyth Yacht Club had capsized and sank, but fortunately this was proved to be untrue by Mr Cyril Kling in his reply to my enquiries.

Being a very densely populated area, as well as our regulars, we had a lot of customers who called at infrequent intervals. One of these was a chap who lived in Daisy Hill; a medium built bloke, who wore a brown suit and a flat brown trilby. He had a red fleshy face, was quiet, and kept to himself. One day he said "Do you keep any money in that safe?" pointing to a big old-fashioned safe, set under the counter at the top of the bar.
I said "Yes, I keep the takings in there."
"I wouldn't if I were you."
"Why ever not?".
He said "I could open that safe in two minutes."
"I'd like to see you," I said.
"If you let me behind the counter, I'll show you," he said.
"OK, come on then, let's see what you can do."
He came behind the counter and took from his inside jacket pocket a leather wallet, about seven or eight inches long. It held a number of thin flat steel instruments. He took out one of these and inserted it into the keyhole of the safe, and in one minute he had the safe open. This shattered my confidence. He could tell by the look on my face that I was worried. "Don't get anxious. I won't do your safe. I never work in this area. All the CID lads in Newcastle would know it was me if I did anything like that around here. I work as far away as Leeds and Manchester whenever there's a job on."
From then on I kept the money upstairs in our flat, a move that I was to regret. A few weeks later it was a busy Friday night. The bar was crowded when in walked three of the local bad lads. One of them had just been released from Wakefield Prison. Emma pointed him out and said "He's just come out of jail."
The three of them were acting over-friendly, full of *bonhomie*, and when Rusty came down from the flat to work in the bar, one of the villains came up to the bar and asked if I could put on a record of Kay Starr singing *Wheel of Fortune*. I sorted the record out and put it on the radiogram. We found out later that this record was the signal to say the coast was clear, As Rusty was down out of the flat, it was standing empty. Their friend waiting outside, shinned up the drainpipe in the back yard and in through a window at the top of the staircase into our flat. Later that night Rusty asked me to go upstairs for some change for the till. I took the keys to open our flat door from the back passage of the pub, but as I opened it I noticed our flat front door was standing wide open. I closed it and went

upstairs. The window on the landing was open and when I switched on the lights I noticed a string of spent matches from the landing into our flat through the living room and into our bedroom, where we kept the takings and our own money. I opened the wardrobe doors and everything was gone, completely cleaned out, not a penny left. I went back downstairs into the bar and quietly told Rusty what had happened. The only other person in the bar I told was a local friend of mine, called Bob Hudson, who lived up Welbeck Road. He was a Fire Officer at Pilgrim Street Fire Station.

He said "You'd better get the police in right away." I phoned Hedlam Street Police Station and they sent down two detectives to make the customary enquiries. As soon as they arrived the customers in the bar just disappeared. After they had conducted their enquiries we were left with one customer, Bob Hudson, and three barmaids. The thieves had got away with about two hundred and thirty-four pounds. That was a lot of money in the '50s. I felt sick. The following day I received a phone call telling me I had to be at Hedlam Street Police Station at 2 pm for an interview with the CID Sergeant. When I went into the interviewing room the Sergeant – a real nasty looking fella – came to the point right away, saying "Did you steal the money?"

I got quite a shock. I was under the impression the police were there to help me. I said "No, I did not. I'm 25 years old, I've just been married and starting out on a career as a successful publican. I have a car standing outside that is worth twelve hundred pounds, which is paid for, by the way. Why should I want to steal two hundred odd pounds?"

He then turned quite nice and said "Well you know, we have to ask these questions." And after a few more questions he thanked me for coming and said he would do what he could, but he had little hope of recovering the money.

In the weeks ahead I did a little detective work myself; that's how I found out about the Kay Starr record as the signal. And I also discovered that most of the money was spent on drink in the *Queen's Head,* Byker, but no definite proof. On the Monday morning I had to phone Mr Norrie at the breweries and inform him of the burglary. He said he would do what he could for me. I was later informed that I would have to go into the office for a meeting with the Big Boss, Colonel Beswick.

The following day I went into the City Road office to see the

Stairway to Paradise with the *Portland* Showgirls.

Congratulating Cissie and Bob Charlton after their sons' 1966 World Cup triumph.

A night out with Rusty in 1967 at the *Queen's Head*, Morpeth, with Arthur Silver and wife Peggy.

Kell with directors and players of Ashington Football Club, 1966. Ron Harrison on left with Louis Johnson; Eric Nichol far right. Seated left Dave Davidson, centre Jack Stafford, right Norman Anderson.

With Northumbrian top policemen and their wives, C. Cooksley (left) and R. Brown.

A Brewery get-together, from left: Kell, Jack Barrass, Norman Thompson, Arthur Silver and a rep.

A kiss from Joan Thirlwell (now Mrs Green) (left) and Joy Allington Warne.

Tyne Tees Television's Ethna Campbell with local photographer and mining official Jack Wallace.

Jock Stein, right, Celtic's manager, brought his team to Portland Park.

We got all the *One O'clock Show* stars at the *Portland*, including Larry Mason.

Sister Dora and dad helped to knock the *Junction* at Widdrington into shape, with Jimmy Jennings.

From right, Davey Ireland, Ian Spencer and Victor Viseur who later took over as manager at the *Portland*.

Jackie Milburn lends a hand

Boss. Colonel Beswick was a huge man, six feet four inches tall and about eighteen stone in weight. He also had a big heart and was most understanding. However, he told me that I should have kept the money in the safe, and I was therefore responsible for the loss. He said he would arrange a repayment figure with Mr Norrie who would let me know how much it would be in due course. It was a nominal amount, two pounds per week, and after a month or two, because the pub was doing so well, Mr Norrie wrote off the loss completely. The money was never recovered, and the thieves were never caught.

The break in had a lasting effect on both of us. Rusty and I felt let down, and I don't think we ever trusted anyone quite the same again. All the regulars were sorry it had happened, but it was soon forgotten and the pub was back into a smooth running routine as if nothing had happened.

The lads and the lasses liked to get out of Walker, even for only a short while, and if anyone mentioned a bus trip to anywhere, you would hear a chorus of "Put my name down." There was always a full bus, especially if we were going to the *Portland*, Ashington. That was a regular trip and my dad and Buck Milburn and all the *Portland* regulars always put on some good entertainment, and made them feel very welcome. The lads from Walker could, and did, reciprocate with some good turns themselves. We had a trip up to Hexham one night to visit Ruth and Garth at the *Fox*. They put on a grand show for us and I had arranged for Buck to meet us at Hexham from Ashington, to play the accordion for the party. After closing time the bus pulled up outside the *Fox* to take us home. We were all outside the pub, waiting to get on the bus, when two of our lads started to fight. The police arrived within minutes. They were still rolling and scuffling about on the ground when the Hexham Sergeant and a constable came up to me and said "Who's in charge of this lot?"

I said "I am."

The Sergeant said "I'll give you ten minutes to get them on the bus and out of Hexham. If you don't I'll lock you up for the night."

I shouted for Curly Wilson to get a couple of the lads to give him a hand to get the two fighters on the bus. Curly, Bob Mulroy and Bob Alcock bundled the battlers onto the bus. One of them had had enough but the other one, Jackie Burke, just wouldn't calm down. So the lads bowled him up the aisle of the bus, threw him on the back seat, and sat on him until he quietened down. We got everyone on the bus with just a few minutes to spare. The Sergeant climbed aboard and shouted "Straight home and don't come back to Hexham."

Another trip we arranged was a visit to Blackpool to see a Blackpool versus Newcastle match. We arrived about ten on the Saturday morning at this charming boarding house in a street just behind the promenade. We were allocated our rooms for our overnight stay and after a wash and brush up we all decided to have a walk along the prom before lunch. When we left for our walk I noticed a nice, large-screen television set in the lounge and numerous pieces of expensive china set out around the rooms and the hallway. When we got back for lunch before going to the match everything had been cleared away, not a thing to be seen. I had a wry smile to myself, but none of the lads noticed. We must have looked a right bunch of roughs. The funny thing is, I would have trusted those lads who were on that trip with my life. I don't remember much about the match. I know it was a capacity crowd; we were in the paddock in front of the season ticket seats and a good number of them seemed to be occupied by Blackpool landladies, the old fashioned kind, dripping with gold and big handbags. Jackie Milburn was playing that day and the Welsh international Ivor Broadis was in the Newcastle team. We all went back to the digs for tea, and that night we were taken by bus to a big pub on the outskirts of Blackpool, where we spent an entertaining evening. The lads all behaved like gentlemen, not a wrong word was spoken. They were perfectly behaved in the boarding house, and when we left on the Sunday, the landlady said "You'll be welcome back any time lads." A great weekend.

One Wednesday I had arranged to pick Bob Alcock up in the MG, to go to a Newcastle game for a 6.00 pm kick off. Bob worked as a welder in the Walker Naval Yard. I arrived at the yard gate just before five and parked the car on a piece of waste ground outside the gate. I got out of the car and walked over to the main gate to wait for Bob. As the hooter went to finish work, about five or six Wolsley police cars screeched to a halt outside the gate and twenty policemen jumped out and started running down the crescent-shaped concrete road which went down to the riverside and the heart of the shipyard. At the same time four thousand shipyard workers were running up the road to get out of the shipyard. I watched as the police and the shipyard workers ran towards each other. As they met, the police were trying to frisk the men at random, but the workers just kept running up the concrete ramp. When the crowd began to disperse I stood and watched the police clearing up an assortment of shipyard equipment. You name it, it was lying there: all sorts of tools, wire lengths, copper piping, brass fittings, electrical fittings, bits of machinery, all strewn over the concrete ramp, all the way down to the heart of the shipyard. Hundreds of pounds worth.

I asked Bob "How often does that happen?"

"Oh, every now and again. It's an accepted part of the job. If the lads see the police they drop anything they're carrying and keep running."

There was no-one arrested, it just seemed to be a game they were playing. Bob and I got in the car and off we went to St James's to watch the match.

For the Queen's Coronation, the breweries had some special presentation glasses made with the head of the Queen and Prince Philip on one side and the Royal Coat of Arms on the other. The quota for my pub was twelve glasses which I was supposed to dish out to my customers. I couldn't show favouritism by giving the glasses to any special customers so I kept the two boxes of six glasses on display on the back fitting of the bar. At that time there was a Royal Naval Auxiliary supply ship in Whigham Richardson's yard for repair and overhaul. Some of the crew were living aboard while she was in for repair. One of them was a gentleman from Goa, a small country on the south west coast of India. This tall, well-built man was the butler on the ship. His father and grandfather had been butlers on board British Naval supply ships before him. A courteous man who was extremely pleasant. He admired the glasses and asked me if I could get any for him to take home to Goa where he said they would be much admired. I told him "I can't get any more as that is my quota, but if they'll be appreciated like that in Goa you can have both boxes as a gift."

He was delighted with the offer and thanked me warmly. The following night be brought me a box filled with all kinds of foodstuffs: a chicken, butter, tea, coffee, chocolates and sweets, which were all in short supply at the time. I thanked him and said there was no need for such kindness. He told me they were sailing the following day, but if he or any of his colleagues were on the Tyne in the future he would send me something for my kindness. He was as good as his word. One night a couple of months later a fellow Goanese butler whose ship was in at North Shields, came up by bus to the *Crown and Anchor* from North Shields with another parcel of goodies with the compliments of his friend. A real gentleman.

One Monday morning Pat the cleaner came in with the news that a ship had put in for repairs at Whigham Richardson's and that the crew were Chinese who were selling contraband cigarettes for two shillings for twenty. Twenty *Players* for two bob. Of course the Chinese and the shipyard lads were getting on like a house on fire. The customs men had combed the ship from stem to stern and hadn't found a thing, yet the Chinese were supplying the shipyard lads with as many tabs as they wished to buy.

That night we got these inscrutable oriental gentlemen in as customers. They came into the bar in twos and threes until we had about thirty of them sitting around the tables, smoking and drinking double Brandys. Only one of them could speak English. He was tall for a Chinese, and wore a sailor's peaked cap. They could all say 'Brandy' and indicated with their fingers how many they wanted. They all sat drinking and smoking with little conversation and not much movement. The bar looked like an oriental opium den. The one with the peaked cap seemed to talk a lot about 'New China' and the shipyard lads soon cottoned on, and every now and then one of the lads would raise his glass to the Chinese and propose: "A toast to New China."

At this, they would all lift their glasses, smile, and drink to New China. This went on for the next few nights and the Chinese seemed to appreciate the hospitality and the music on the radiogram. I recalled having a record I had swapped with a Greek seaman a few weeks earlier. The label had oriental hieroglyphics on it so I sorted it out and put it on for the benefit of the Chinese. No response. Not a dicky bird. So I asked the one with the peaked cap, who seemed to be the boss, "Don't you like Chinese music?"

He said "Not Chinese music – Japanese music." I crawled back into my shell.

The shipyard lads weren't really worried about New China or Mao-Tse-Tung or General Chaing Kai Chek. China was a hell of a long way from Low Walker in the 1950s, and as long as the lads had a job to do in the shipyard, they were quite willing to make any of the nationalities of seamen welcome whenever their ships called for repair or refit. It was work for them and that's all they really worried about. Politics was the last thing on their minds. They were renowned for building the best ships in the world and took great pride in that. Full employment on the Tyne, made for a happy and prosperous Geordie.

Not all the lads in Walker were canny lads, there were one or two villains. One in particular I remember rang the bell of our flat one afternoon about 4.00 pm. When I answered the door he was standing there, a small lad with brown wavy hair, in his twenties. He said "Is Larry Seaman in?"

"No, he's finished here now and I'm the new manager."

He said "Oh. Well, I've been away at sea for the last few months and I didn't know he'd left. When I come back I usually bring Larry one or two things back, like nylons and shirts and some foodstuffs, butter and eggs and things like that."

I said "I don't know where he is now, I'm sorry."

He said "Would you be interested in them?"

I invited him upstairs to talk about what he had. He said he had the nylons aboard ship which was berthed at the *Neptune Yard*. He told me that the ship's cook actually had them and the foodstuff and he would have to take the ready money to get them from him.

I smelt a rat, and said "If you bring the goods here I'll pay you for them."

He said no that wouldn't do, as he would have to take the money first to get them from the ship's cook. "If you don't trust me then you can come down and wait for me at the gate, and I'll also give you my club membership card with my name and address in it to prove I'm honest."

I said "How much will you want?"

"About thirty pounds should cover it."

I said "I've only got twenty-four pounds."

He said "Well, that'll do."

"Right, I'll take you down in the car and I'll wait for you outside the gate."

We went down to the *Neptune Yard* and I parked the car outside Tommy Hannigan's shop, opposite the *Neptune Hotel*. He got out and walked towards the shipyard gate and I sat and waited for him to return with the stuff. I waited, and waited, but he never showed. I waited until a quarter to six and realised I'd been done. I went back home and told Rusty he had done off with the money and all we had to show for it was his Working Men's Club book. The name and address on the front of the book was fictitious, but on looking through the book I found in one of the back leaves a name and address written in a child's hand. This was his *real* address.

I told some of the lads in the bar what had happened: Kenny, Curly, Bob, Jackie, Shorty and Tommy. They knew his address and said they would put the frighteners on him to pay me the money back. We arranged to go up one night after the pubs closed to give him enough time to get home then pay him a call. The night was arranged and Kenny, Jackie and Shorty went with me in the MG to try and get hold of him. We parked the car a few yards from the house. Kenny and Jackie went up and knocked on the door. They asked if they could have a word with him about a job. He came to the back garden gate to have a word and Kenny and Jackie grabbed him and bundled him into the car and off we went down to the *Crown and Anchor* where Curly, Bob, and Tommy were waiting with Rusty in the bar.

We carried him into the bar and sat him down on a bench seat. I then began to grill him about the money and the story he had told me. He admitted he had conned me, but he promised on "God's Honour," that he would pay me back. He was as white as a ghost and kept asking for a glass of water. I asked him how much money he had on him, and he turned out his pockets. He had about twenty-four shillings. I took that and put it in my pocket, realising that was all we were going to get from him. I took him out to the car and with one or two of the lads we took him for a ride. We went down through Wallsend and at Howden we pushed him out of the car and told him to walk home – no buses, no taxis, a long walk. I never received the remainder of the money, but I'll bet he'll think twice before trying that trick on again in Walker.

The following day I was in Matty Harvey's shop and I told Matty about what had happened. He said "You know, Bill, that's like taking the law into your own hands. If he goes to the police you could get into trouble."

I said "He won't go to the police, he's a bloody villain." I never saw the man again, but Kenny had called into a pub with his wife one night, in Newcastle, and had seen him sitting with a couple of his mates. Kenny had made a strategical withdrawal before anything started, and he told me that night when he got back to the *Crown and Anchor*, he knew how the other fellow had felt, when we had hold of him.

When we were at the *Crown and Anchor*, Rusty and I met a great number of people, both in and out of the trade. One man was called Wilf Hope, about 60 years old, white hair, a figure like Falstaff and a voice to match. He was manager of the *Peartree Hotel* in Felling. His voice was so huge he didn't have to shout time, he just announced it. We became good friends. The *Peartree*, like the *Crown and Anchor* was a *McEwans* Brewery pub and as managers for the same firm we tried to drum up business for each other. Wilf would arrange a bus load of his customers to come over to us for a darts match with sandwiches, or a sing song on one of our quiet nights, and I would do the same with a trip to his pub a fortnight later. It was a change for the customers and they all enjoyed it. Wilf's wife always put on a good spread of food for us: home-baked plate pies, sausage rolls, everything beautifully made. She was Wilf's anchor, a hard worker, who always made you feel welcome. A grand lass. They kept a family pub, and all their locals knew they would get a sympathetic hearing from Wilf and his wife whenever they had any troubles, or needed help.

Another couple of pals we met, of all places, at Leeds United Football Ground at a Newcastle Cup replay. It was a midweek game and next to us in the crowd were a couple of middle-aged men, who said they came from High Pit, Cramlington. They were Bill Johnson and Bob Hymers. Bill was steward of the High Pit Club and Bob was secretary of the club. I told them I was in the trade and managed a pub in Walker. Bob said "That's a coincidence; we'll have to come over to see you one night."

And sure enough, they did, and we became good friends. They were soon regular visitors to the *Crown and Anchor*, and Rusty and I often popped in to see them at the High Pit Club. Bob Hymers spent the next thirty years building up the High Pit to what it is today. He died of a heart attack after chasing some youths who were stealing from a dray delivery wagon. Bob devoted his whole life to the smooth running of the High Pit Club.

Another couple who became good friends were George and Eva Pearson. I met them at the *Harmonic Hall*, Ashington, while I was running an outside catering bar for David Absolom who was running the *Harmonic* as a dance and function hall. George and Eva had been invited to a party organised by David for the cast of a pantomime that was playing at the *Palace Theatre* in the Haymarket, Newcastle. David was a partner in the *Palace Theatre Company*, and had decided to give the whole cast a party in the *Harmonic*. They were all bussed through to Ashington after the show. Most of them were still wearing their makeup when they arrived. Larry Grayson was the star of the show and my job was to see that the principals of the show were well looked after with drinks. George and Eva were friends of the stars. I thought they were in the show, so they got special treatment too. George and Eva had some of their own friends with them and they all received star treatment from me.

In the course of the evening they found out that I had a pub in Walker so George and Eva and their friends said they would all come down to see me. They usually did their drinking at the *Brandling Arms*, Brandling Village, in Gosforth, and also spent some time at the *Aero Club* in Newcastle. They were a colourful crowd. Handsome men and beautiful women. One of the men in the group was called Eddie Farnon, small, finely built, dark hair and dark eyes with aquiline features, like a Spanish Nobleman. He moved like a gymnast, always immaculately dressed. Eddie and George were regular visitors to our pub. Eddie helped his brother run a big store in Newcastle with the motto *Try Farnons First*. He drove a *Rolls Royce* and whenever he and George called to see me they would invite me for a run down to the coast. I couldn't always accept their hospitality because of the business, but when I did we used to go down to the *Rex Hotel* Buffet for a drink. Whitley Bay had a summertime extension of hours which meant the pubs were open until 11 pm. At that time the *Rex* had one of the best barmen in the North East. His name was Jeff Murphy, who sported a large handlebar moustache; a good cocktail man, always very pleasant, a ready wit, and could talk about anything. It was always a pleasure to watch him at work. We used to call in at North Shields and visit the pubs down in the Low Lights; there was always something entertaining going on down there. The two pubs we frequented were *The Fleece* and *The Northumberland Arms* which was better known as *The Jungle*. *The Fleece* always had a little man who wore a black Homburg hat; he sat on a stool playing the accordion. He had a boxer's face with a cigarette dangling permanently out of the side of his mouth. The place was always busy; plenty of ships and seamen in Shields in the '50s. *The Jungle* was run in those days by a Maltese who catered mainly for the sailors. He had a piano player in the side room who was always worth a visit. He sported a Paderewsky haircut and looked like Max Wall. He liked you to request some classical piano piece like *Poet and Peasant*, that he could really get his teeth into. In the course of the recital he would strip the piano of everything but the keyboard. He used to knock hell out of it. A real pub piano player. *The Jungle* in Shields was known by sailors throughout the world.

The Traveller's Rest, Blyth

Our stay at the *Crown and Anchor* was drawing to a close. One day late in '53 Mr Norrie called and told me that the Breweries had thoughts of promotion for me and would I be interested in taking a much bigger pub in Blyth? *The Traveller's Rest*. The pub had three separate departments – Bar, Buffet, and Lounge, and the Breweries wanted me to learn how to control three separate stocks in the one pub which would give me the experience to perhaps move on to better things in the future. I knew the pub, and after talking it over with Rusty we told him we would take it.

The changeover went smoothly. A couple called Mr and Mrs Jack McBride were chosen to take over the *Crown and Anchor* and the pair who had been managing the *Traveller's Rest*, a Mr and Mrs Clafton, were to move to Whitley Bay to take over the *Ship Hotel*.

The Claftons had been popular with the customers, and the staff at the *Traveller's Rest* and we inherited both when we took over the pub. Most pub managers will agree that it is easy to take over a place that has been badly run by a disinterested manager. But it is difficult to take over from a manager who has been on top of the job and kept things running smoothly. So Rusty and I had to play our cards close to our chests for the first few weeks. The staff consisted of two full-time barmaids: Florence in the Buffet Bar and Peggy in the Main Bar. Jimmy and Tommy were part-time barmen with Jackie and Barbara Thompson. Barbara was also the cleaner and part-time barmaid, and Jackie, her husband, was the General Factotum of the place, also engaged as a full-time bookie's runner by Mr Waters of Blyth. Jackie took all the bets at the *Traveller's Rest* and surrounding streets. His office was the bottle and jug, just off the main bar. Jackie's other job was part-time waiter and concert chairman. There were no betting shops in those days and Mr Waters had most of the back street betting in Blyth all tied up. A very rich man. John Bell was our piano player who played three nights a week. The Bar and the Buffet did outstanding business. The takings were consistent, but the lounge was 'hitty missy'. It needed a little organisation. It was open at weekends and an odd night during the week for darts matches, otherwise it stayed closed. Rusty and I decided to try a Tuesday night concert. We asked the piano player if he was willing to have a go and he was all for it. I suggested we engage one artiste – a semi-professional – as the main entertainment. I knew the local lads and lasses would be willing to get up and sing a song to fill in the programme. One little lad we could always depend on was Tommy Wright, a good entertainer who did all of Johnnie Ray's songs such as *Cry, All of Me, Such a Night*, and *Walkin' my Baby Back Home*.

I was allowed to pay the artiste thirty shillings by the Brewery, which was about the going rate at the time. We usually booked a good singer or comedian. George Meredith was a regular booking and Jimmy Munro from West Sleekburn was a real good local comedian, just a pit lad, but with rare talent for making people laugh. There were some good singers in the district who we could call on, and some of our regular bookings were lads like the Millican Brothers, Bob and Alan. Tommy Nesbitt was another popular singer, a great ballad singer. Tommy Nesbitt and Alan Millican became national stars on TV twenty-five years later as *Millican and Nesbitt*; but they sang for me for thirty shillings a night and were quite happy with the money. Two canny lads.

Some good singers came over from Ashington to help me out: Donnie Alsopp was a regular and appealed to his audience who liked the songs he sang. There were also a group from Ashington called *The Five Beaux and a Belle*. I couldn't afford to book them as a group, but they all came over to Blyth and sang for me individually. Dickie Slaughter was their piano player and he occasionally came over to accompany each of the singers, free gratis, just for the night out. At that time Lillian Browell was the *Belle* of the group. She had a beautiful voice, and was popular with the audience. The lads were Alan Richardson, Bill Jordan and Ben Cherrington. Eric Nichol was the comic of the group. All good turns in their own right. Over the years, some of the Belles were replaced with singers like Lillian Turner, Audrey Robinson and Doris Pearson, all wonderful vocalists.

Another group from Hunwick in Durham promised they would come and give us a free show. It was a Concert Party run by a couple of our friends, from the days Rusty had spent in Hunwick. They were Ossie Rae and Totty Sleeth. The party included a busty, blond lady singer and two other artistes, all good entertainers. A date was arranged for the show and they duly arrived, if rather late. They had got lost on their way to Blyth from Hunwick. They arrived about 9 pm so we had to revise the show accordingly. By 10 pm they were only half way through the show, so I suggested to the customers that if they drank off, we would carry on with the show. Everyone agreed so the show went on.

The highlight was Ossie and Totty's Hypnosis Act. They put one or two of the customers under the influence and had them doing all sorts of things they wouldn't normally do. They had one women from Ashington lying as flat as a board across the backs of two chairs and proceeded to stick pins and needles in her arms and legs. The man she was with came over to me in an agitated state and said "She's with me but she's not my wife. I've only got the loan of her for the night. When she gets home her man'll want to know where she's got all those holes in her arms from."

To calm him I asked Ossie and Totty to refrain and bring her out of the trance. They sat her on a chair and with a snap of the fingers they brought her out of the trance. She awoke as right as rain to the sound of applause. The show was a huge success and as the customers were leaving we had a visit from a local bobby on the beat. Somebody had reported to him that we had a lounge full of customers nearly an hour after closing time. He wanted to know what was going on. He was a young chap, probably straight out of Hendon Police College and he was obviously keen to collar somebody. I explained what had happened and when I told him about the show he said "I believe that practising hypnosis in a public place is against the law."

I couldn't argue with him because I didn't know the law with regard to hypnosis.

He said "I would like you to accompany me to the station with whoever is in charge of the Concert Party, to make a statement."

Ossie volunteered to go with me to Blyth Police Station. He did everything with theatrical flourish: a typical pantomime dame and his lifelong dream was to work on the stage. In reality he was an insurance man in Hunswick. Ossie was a compassionate, kind man, and a good friend to Rusty and me. He was most upset at having to go to the Police Station to make a statement. Not so much for himself, but worried in case it would get Rusty and me into trouble with the Breweries. He kept saying "I'm very sorry, Mr Kell, to get

The Traveller's Rest, Blyth

you into all this bother."

However, we both made our statements and we were allowed to leave the Police Station about 1 am. I asked if I could use the phone to call Rusty to come and pick us up in the car, and, within a few minutes, we were back at the *Traveller's* where the rest of the Concert Party were waiting to find out what had happened. After making my statement I was told that myself and Mrs Kell would have to present ourselves at 11 am the following morning for an interview with Superintendent J. D. Patterson. Ossie and the Concert Party had some supper and left for a long deflated journey back to Hunwick, Co. Durham.

The following morning Rusty and I went along to Bridge Street Police Station for our meeting with the Superintendent. We were both worried as to the outcome. After a short wait we were shown into his office. It was a large room with a high ceiling, high narrow windows where the morning sun streamed through onto a very large old-fashioned desk, at which the Superintendent was sitting. He welcomed us and asked us to sit down. J. D. Patterson was a good copper and he knew everything that was going on in Blyth. He knew quite a lot about us through a mutual friend called Tommy Bridson. Tommy had worked with Rusty in the Tax Office in Morpeth and, when he visited J. D. in Blyth, they both used to call into the *Traveller's* for a drink and a chat with Rusty.

J. D. opened the interview. "What's this I hear about you?"

We were both eager to explain what had happened. After listening to our explanation, he sat thinking for a while and, with the trace of a smile on his face, he said, "I have no objection to you getting your customers under the influence of alcohol, but I do object to you putting them under the influence of hypnosis. I think we can take it that this case is closed and you won't be hearing any more about it."

He showed us out of his office and said "Good morning Mr and Mrs Kell, and I don't want to see you here again."

We thanked him and left, feeling very relieved. J. D. Patterson had a great deal of sympathy and understanding for the Licenced Victuallers of Blyth, also his wife's people, whose maiden name was Clark, had kept the *Black Bull* in Bridge Street, Morpeth for a good number of years in the 1940s. Thereafter each Licence issued at the Annual Licence Meeting in February, (The Brewster Sessions) had a printed notice attached to it saying "Hypnosis is not allowed to be practised in any public place without a Licence." That was the outcome of our meeting with the Superintendent.

Blyth was a busy place in the early '50s. The Port of Blyth had dozens of ships coming and going every week, exporting coal to the Scandinavian countries and importing timber from the same countries. A number of coastal colliers took coal from Blyth to London and most of their crews were local men. The coal trimmers were working at full capacity and were the top paid men working in the Port of Blyth at that time. The shipyard was also busy. I remember they had to extend the slipway to build a ship called *The William J. Walkley* for an Australian Company. The bow of that ship was towering right above the *Traveller's Rest* while she was being built. The shipyard was working day and night. *Hughes Bolckow* the ship breaker's yard was also working at full capacity, breaking up all kinds of ships: Liners, Battleships, Submarines, all sorts.

Hughes Bolckow's yard was on the Cambois side of the river, and many of the lads working there had to use the old chain ferry to go to and fro across the river from Blyth. There were some grand bargains to be picked up at *Bolckows*, especially when they were breaking up an old luxury liner. Beautiful wood panelling, furnishings, and ship's furniture. Their showroom was an *Alladin's Cave* of ships' paraphernalia, all beautifully made by craftsmen and all at scrap prices.

We had a mixture of customers. There were seamen, deep sea and coastal; shipyard workers; miners from Bates and Cambois pit across the river; local businessmen; and ship's officers who frequented the buffet bar and room.

It was a popular pub, and they kept us busy. One bustling Friday night, Jackie Thompson, who was working as waiter and concert chairman in the lounge, came running into the bar and shouted to me that somebody was threatening to hit Rusty. I ran through to the lounge and saw a man in his shirt sleeves banging on the counter with his fists and shouting abuse at Rusty and the barmaid. I didn't ask any questions, just grabbed his shoulder, spun him around and hit him hard with a right hook. He stumbled back across the room, fell against the lounge door and slumped to the floor. I ran to ask Rusty if she was OK. She said "Yes, I'm alright." A couple of lads

The Traveller's Rest, Blyth

lifted him up and took him outside and everything carried on as normal. we didn't have any trouble with him again. In fact, we had no more trouble of that nature for the rest of the time we spent at the *Traveller's*.

Staff. Now there's a thing. What every publican hopes for in his staff is honesty and loyalty. Not easy to come by these days. But in the '50s it was a much more common virtue. Honesty was easier to find especially among the older barmaids. Loyalty? Well, you had to work at that a little harder. Loyalty works both ways. Once the staff know they can trust you, then with any luck, they give their loyalty to you. In our 36 years in the trade together, Rusty and I have been lucky with our staff, and I can count on one hand the villains who have robbed us. And they will know if they are reading this who I mean. I wonder if it did them any good? But business is business and that's the risk you take when it's a ready cash transaction. We were furtunate at the *Traveller's*. We never had any trouble with stock shortages.

After a year at Blyth, I had a phone call from Mr Winder, who was the head man at City Road in charge of the Managed Houses section of the Breweries. He asked me if I would be willing to take over the Management of the *Portland Hotel* at Ashington. Norman Winder was a quiet spoken man who had worked in the City Road office all his life. He had worked his way up from being an office boy. My first reaction when I received his call was to say "What about my father?"

Norman replied "Your father has no say in the matter. We will get him a smaller house to manage. If *you* don't take the *Portland*, we will get someone else. We would like you in charge because you know the pub and we know you can improve its potential."

I said "I will let you know my decision as soon as possible."

"We'll give you a day or two to think about it." he said. "But we'll need a definite answer as soon as possible."

What a predicament to be in. That afternoon I went through to Ashington to see my father. He had already heard from Norman Winder by phone and he wasn't best pleased. He had called Norman some choice names. After 20 years with the Breweries it wasn't a nice way to be treated. Eventually a compromise was reached and dad agreed to go back to his old pub in Gateshead, *The*

Gloucester Inn, High West Street. My dad had been a top manager for the Breweries in the 30s and 40s, one of their 'Blue Eyed Boys', but now he was getting older and not as fit as he had been. They were giving him the elbow. I made up my mind then that I would never give them the opportunity to do that to me when I got nearer sixty.

My father put on a brave face when he moved back to Gateshead, but it was a hell of a comedown for him and he must have felt bitter about it. My parents made the best of it and a lot of their old customers went back to the *Gloucester* to see them. As the months went by, the hurt softened and they enjoyed their time at the 'Old' *Gloucester*. Many of their old friends were still in Gateshead: Joe and Annie Blakeborough, Sally Jennings, Lizzie Shields and her sister Rosie and a host of others. My dad's old barman Kit Stoddart travelled from Ashington to Gateshead every weekend to give him a hand behind the bar. Kit had never been married and he looked on my parents as his family. Now there's loyalty for you.

Blyth had a good shopping centre with an influx of customers on market days from all the surrounding pit villages. It was also a good place for what the pit lads called 'a day on the beer'. Pubs galore, all the way down Regent Street, around the market place, right down to the Port of Blyth. They would spend all morning going from pub to pub, and at 3.00 pm, closing time, they'd visit one of a number of cafés for a meal, then back on the beer at six, opening time. Before catching the bus home, they usually ended up in one of three pubs that accommodated 'Ladies of Easy Virtue': the *Fox and Hounds*, *Dun Cow*, and the *Commercial Inn*. What we would call today 'Exotic Entertainment'. The going rate for a 'short-time' was thirty bob...and no tick!

Blyth also had an active Licensed Victuallers' Association under chairman Stan Gray who had the *Station Hotel*. The official title of the organisation was 'The Blyth and Morpeth LVA'. Stan Gray ensured that everyone abided by the rules. No-one was allowed to get away with any unfair trading.

He called to see me one morning. "Noo then, Bill, Aa've got it on good authority that ye've been givin' away meat pies in your pub."

"Aye, that's right, Stan, but only on concert nights."

"Noo, Bill, Aa knaa you're new to the game, but that gans right against the rules of wor LVA."

"Aa knaa, Stan, but if Aa hadn't given 'em away they would've gone off by the next mornin'."

"Whey, we'll let it gan this once, but Aa have to give ye an official warnin' that ye mustn't ever do that sort of thing in the future."

Blyth LVA was a close-knit circle and no member was allowed to step out of line. I made a mental note to keep the rules for the rest of my stay in Blyth.

Back to the *Portland*, 1955

We moved back to the *Portland* three weeks before Easter, 1955. The Breweries had hired Jack Steadman to take over the *Traveller's*. After handing the keys over, we wished him luck and headed back to Ashington.

The *Portland* was a real challenge, a great big ghoustie pub that had had little done to it since 1939. When we took over it still had the blackout curtains which had been used during the war; and nicotine-stained walls; and ceilings with dark brown wooden surrounds. The lino was turning up at the edges with old age, revealing large holes, worn with the constant shuffling of miners' feet.

Rusty's sister Lily and her husband Bob Weatherston came to help us to get things in order. The lino was considered too dangerous so we just pulled it up, threw it out, and left the bare floorboards to be scrubbed clean.

McEwan's and my father had been depending on the quality of the beer to sell the product for a long time, but the public wanted something more: comfortable surroundings and plush seating, clean and ventilated rooms, as well as a good pint of beer.

Rusty and I set about trying to give them just that. It was like getting blood out of a stone trying to convince the Breweries to spend any money on improving the pub. We simply had to use what little we were given to do what we thought best at the time. The customers appreciated that and the business began to improve. The takings were going up every week. New blood, a few new ideas and lots of enthusiasm gave the *Portland* a new lease of life.

Rusty's older sister, Joyce and her husband Tommy Davies, came in to help. And the enthusiasm was infectious as far as the rest of the staff were concerned. They were all mad keen to see the pub go well. My dad's old barmen who had stayed on were all pleased to see the *Portland* get back into top gear again. Jimmy Thompson, Jimmy Locke and Alfie Imber all worked hard to bring this about. We still had the same cleaners who had worked for my father:

Nancy Robinson, her sister Jean and her daughter, Joyce; all three dependable as a *Rolls Royce*.

We also inherited my father's entertainers: *The Band*, Joe Kelly on drums; Billy Oliver accordion; Sammy Freeman accordion; and Ken Hayes piano. Little Billy Todd was acting unpaid Concert Chairman. The Band played Friday night, Saturday night and Sunday morning for the *Jolly Boys* and they received four pounds per week between them. That worked out at a pound apiece for the whole weekend. They enjoyed playing together, while a full house and a round of applause did wonders for their ego. They spent more on their beer than they received in wages. But you could get a lot of beer those days at one and tuppence a pint. You could buy four gallons of beer and forty cigarettes for around four pounds.

Little Billy Todd, the concert chairman, had authority in his announcements, a gravelly sort of voice, the voice of command. When he asked anyone to get up and sing a song they automatically rose and sang their hearts out. He always had plenty of support from his three brothers: Tommy, Albert and Jimmy, the youngest. They could all sing a good song with fine strong voices. Donnie Alsopp was the vocalist with the band, and he sang with them every weekend. They were all miners, working hard through the week, and at the weekends they liked a drink and a bit pleasure. They made their own entertainment. Very few had television in '55 so they spent their nights at the pub or club, or at the pictures.

All the collieries were working to full capacity in and around Ashington: Woodhorn, North Seaton, Linton, New Moor, Ellington, Lynemouth and Pegswood, and Newbiggin was still going at that time. Full employment. What ecstasy. And no strikes. Plenty of money to spend for those who were willing to work hard. A lot of people were resentful of the big money the miners were making, but I wasn't. They were spending a lot of it in my pub, so I was quite happy with the situation. Ashington was a boom town and I made my mind up I would take full advantage of every opportunity to make as much money as possible while the boom lasted. Selling beer was my job, and the more I sold the happier the Breweries were, which gave me more bargaining power when I wanted them to spend any money on my ideas to improve the potential of the pub. It was a gradual, slow process, but we were winning.

Rusty was pregnant when we took over the *Portland* but she

carried on working right up until she was due to have the baby. In the meantime she taught Peggy Wilson how to manage the Buffet Bar, to take over when the baby came along. And in the bar we employed a big blond Irish woman called Olive Hamill with the help of a couple of young girls, Joan and Margaret, to run the main bar. They were all full-time staff, and at weekends we had a nucleus of part-timers to fill in on busy nights. We were selling 14 Hogsheads of beer a week at that time, what they now call Real Ale, and I did all the cellar work myself, I didn't like anyone interfering with my routine in the cellar. The spiling was done by the draymen and the rest was left to me. I tapped all the casks when needed and made sure the beer was in 'tip top' condition when required. There were 17 beer pumps to keep clean every week, so the cellar was a full-time job.

Sunday morning was always busy and we used to fill dozens of pints of beer ready for opening when they all rushed in at twelve o'clock. We had a Jolly Boys Club sing song on Sunday morning and the local bookies' runners paid out the Saturday's winning bets in the bar on a Sunday morning. It all made for a busy time. The taking of bets in a public house was, and still is illegal, but it was done with subtlety, and I wasn't supposed to see anyone making wagers. If it got too blatant I would have a quiet word and everything went undercover for a while.

Our daughter Leonie Cheralyn Kell was born in the No. 1 bedroom at the *Portland Hotel* on Sunday morning at 10.00 am on November 6th, 1955. Everything had gone well; no complications. Doctor J. J. Hobbs, with the aid of the local midwife, delivered Leonie with no problems. Rusty was fine.

I told Olive and all the Sunday morning staff as they came into work that we now had a daughter. They were all chuffed to ribbons to hear the news, and it was arranged *not* to tell the customers until they were all in, served and settled. They they could tell the customers of the birth and give them all a drink on the house, to wet the baby's head. When the announcement was made there was a stampede for the bar. It wasn't every day they got a free drink out of *Kell*. Those who were drinking halves ordered pints; those drinking pints ordered large rums, or large whiskies; many ordered a cigar to go with the free drink. One thing about the pit lads, they knew how to take advantage of you. It cost me £34 for that round of drinks; exactly three weeks' wages, at that time. The Buffet wasn't open on a Sunday morning, so on the Sunday night I had a delegation, headed by Jackie Swalwell, to ask about *their* free drinks. So more cigars and free drinks were flowing in the Buffet which cost me another £15. What a day. Rusty was up and about by tea time that Sunday and that evening she did the books and the staff wages for me. What a woman.

Ashington then was a town of approximately 28,000 people with an Urban District Council. Both Rusty and I spent most of our formative years there. Our families were well known in the community. So we knew and were known by most of the people in Ashington at that time. All our old friends were pleased to see us back at the *Portland*. We knew all the canny folk and we also knew all the funny buggers so we had a good head start in the business of running a big pub. What the drinkers of Ashington wanted was a good pint of beer; a good singer; good music; and a good laugh. And they laughed mainly at themselves. I remember Walter Lawson who owned most of the cinemas in Ashington putting on the film *Henry the Fifth* with Lawrence Olivier at the Regal Cinema. Nobody went! He had to take it off on the Wednesday night and replace it with an Abbott and Costello film to recoup his losses. That told me something about Ashington that I have kept to myself for years.

It took just over a year to get the pub into a reasonable condition. The Breweries redecorated and refurbished the whole of the downstairs. New curtains, new lino, and repainted throughout, which included the main Bar, the Back Bar, the Buffet, the Singing Room and the Five End Room which we renamed The Starters Room. That's where most of the young lads in Ashington started drinking. It had bench seats, lino on the floor and tables with two or three stools at each. I put a Juke Box in and a set of weight-lifting gear to keep them occupied. It was extremely popular. The young lads always ordered pints when they first started drinking; a man's drink. But the beer in those days soon sorted the men out from the boys. They used to get into some bonny states and were usually carried home.

After we had the downstairs up and running smoothly, Rusty started on the upstairs. At the head of the main staircase were three average-sized rooms and a large dining room which had never been used for years. They had been storage rooms for my father and were still full of junk he had collected over all the years he had spent there. Things he had taken as payment for debts his customers had incurred. There were all sorts: oil paintings, water colours, jugs, ornaments, sets of drums, accordions, a bass fiddle, suits, overcoats, fur coats, all kinds of hats: women's hats, men's hats, caps and about twenty bowler hats. In the old days my dad used to lend them out for funerals. Old swords and spears, shot guns, stone jars covered with basket weave that the whisky and rum used to be delivered in. Old furniture, chairs, stools, hat racks, sideboards, books, magazines, papers, postcards, old bill heads, letters, old records (78s) some by Layton and Johnson, The Street Singer, and Gracie Fields, and *In a Monastery Garden* which was a must to any record collection before the war.

Rusty threw the whole lot out. The bin men were wearing bowler hats for weeks.

The rooms looked bare and empty after Rusty was finished with them, but they were next on the agenda for use and development.

Our first year in the *Portland* had been an eventful one: a noteworthy year. We now had a lovely little daughter; we were both busy running the business which was improving every week; and we were more than happy doing our job.

Newcastle United had won the FA Cup again that year (1955) and a few weeks after Leonie was born Jackie Milburn brought the FA Cup through to the *Portland* to let the lads have a look at it. All the staff had their photos taken holding the Cup and we had one of Leonie taken at a few weeks old sitting inside it. The Cup was on display for three weeks and just about every one of the customers had their photograph taken beside it.

Through the week we had our regular morning customers, usually the pitmen on the night shift. They would call in for a couple of pints and put on a bet, then back home to bed. In the evening we had our regulars who were from all walks of life in the town. Amongst these there were a number of Ashington characters. One, a hard-up, self-employed upholsterer who always wore a flat brimmed *Attaboy* Trilby hat and a black semi-fitting thirty bob top coat. All the customers and staff knew him as *Oosh ye Bugger*. He called in every morning and checked all the seats for any damage then reported to me any in need of repair. I gave him a job occasionally which only cost me a few shillings. The seats were kept in perfect condition. On a hot day he would walk into the bar, take off his trilby, wipe his brow and say "Oosh ye Bugger, Bill, it's

Back to the Portland, 1955

hot." On a cold day he would walk in and go up to the coal fire and warm his hands and say "Oosh ye Bugger, Bill it's cold." He got a part-time job waiting-on at a club called *The Kicking Cuddy*. It was a men-only club. After Jimmy had served him with a drink, one of the customers asked him if he would pop next door to Porky Ehrmann's to get him a ninepenny pork sandwich. Jimmy agreed and held his hand out for the money and the customer said "Here's another ninepence, get one for yourself."

A few minutes later Jimmy Oosh ye Bugger walked in eating a pork sandwich and said to the customer "Here's your ninepence back; they only had one left. Oosh ye Bugger."

Titchie Smith was another Ashington character, as quiet as a mouse when he was sober, but as soon as he'd had a few drinks, he started speaking with a loud American accent. A cocky little chap, always getting into the way of somebody's fist. As soon as one black eye had cleared up he acquired another one.

Early one Friday night about 7 pm before the bar got busy, old Ned Bell was sitting in his usual wooden armchair beside the fire in the bar, when in came Titchie. He'd obviously had a few. He walked up to Old Ned and said in his loud American accent, "Hi there, you old sod. How you keeping?" and tilted old Ned's cap off over the back of his head.

Old Ned had a short fuse to start with and I could see he was upset. Ned suffered from a back injury in the pit and couldn't stand up straight. He said to Titchie, "A few years ago I would have knocked your bloody head off for doing that."

When I saw what was happening I lifted the counter flap and walked up behind Titchie and put my arms around him, pinning his arms down by his sides. I bent his body forward towards Old Ned and said "Go on. Hit him Ned."

Ned hit him hard on the chin two or three times from his seat to give vent to his feelings. When Ned had finished I let Titchie go and said to him "That'll teach you to interfere with my customers." Titchie never said a word. He blinked his eyes open wide, shook his head and walked away up to the middle of the long bar and asked for a pint. We didn't get another squeak out of him all night. Old Ned Bell had been a hard lad in his younger days. He had fought with the Royal Naval Division at the Dardanelles in the First World War. I enjoyed listening to his yarns about the old days. He could have written a book about his life. It would have been most interesting.

Old Sally Gladson was another mazer and one of our regular customers. She liked a gill of beer and she always smoked a clay pipe. Always dressed in black. Hat: black, usually with a big pin in it. Long black dress with a black pinny and a black coat and black laced-up high boots. She had brought up a big family and was a staunch member of the Labour Party; an active supporter. They all sent for Sally if their bairns were sick, or anyone in the family had died. She was always there to help. A grand old girl.

There were dozens of customers who were regulars at the *Portland*, and a pleasure to serve. Old Bill Robertson always had a smile and a kind word; Old Andy Hay and his pal Geordie Bryson; Old Bill Thompson who had won the Military Medal in the First World War and had three beautiful red-headed daughters, a canny old chap; Old Hess Morris and his brother Matty; Bob Patterson; Jimmy Thompson the barber; Walter Beddow the Fish Shop Man; Little Davey Grant, a canny little Scotsman; Jack Hamilton who wouldn't harm a fly. All canny folk. Susie Dawson and her sister Ivy, who were our regulars in the Buffet; Elsie Cobb who married the son of a Lord, Basil Cobb, stationed in Ashington during the war with the Northumberland Fusiliers. I remember Elsie spent her honeymoon in Paris and she brought me an expensive silk tie back as a present. I kept it for years. It's a pleasure remembering them all.

Jimmy Thompson the barber came in one morning and walked up to the bar, saying "I'm a bit short of cash Bill, could you change a *Bradbury* for me?"

I asked "What is it?"

"It's one of the first pound notes issued after the gold sovereigns were withdrawn as currency."

"Why a *Bradbury*?" I asked.

"They named it after the Chief Cashier who signed them."

I took it from him and gave him a pound note out of the till. Another little piece of history.

A well-known and respected character was a gentle Scotsman called Jim MacKintosh, Ashington's Chief Inspector of Police, an old pal of my dad. He proved to be a great friend to me during my stay as manager at the *Portland*. Jim came from a small village between Elgin and Nairn on the north-east coast of Scotland to join the Northumberland Police Force in the early part of the war. He was acting Sergeant at Ashington in 1940 then went to Morpeth and was promoted to Sergeant. From Morpeth he went to Newburn on Tyne. He told me the tale about another well-known character in the Northumberland Force, whose name was Jack Cattermole. Jack was detailed to watch an outcrop of coal that the locals had been taking, up past the *Frenchman's Arms* on the West Road. His shift finished at 10 pm and he had arranged with his relief to arrive early to give him time to get down to the *Frenchman's Arms* for a couple of pints. Jack loved a pint. One night the relief and the landlord of the pub played a joke on Jack. The relief Constable deliberately arrived late on the job to relieve Jack. Jack peddalled his bike like mad to catch the pub, but when he got there it was closed and in darkness. He knocked on the door and the landlord opened the upstairs window to ask who it was. Jack, who was all hot and bothered and thirsty, said. "Can you let me have a couple of pints? I'm dying for a drink."

The landlord said, "OK," and came down in the dark, opened the door and let Jack into the pitch black passage. The landlord handed Jack a pint who swallowed it down in one go; it never touched the sides. Jack said, "Can I have another one?" and the landlord obliged. Half way down the second pint Jack stopped drinking and said "Ye bugger, that's waater!"

And the landlord said "So was the first one."

Jim MacKintosh returned to Ashington as Inspector in 1949 and was promoted to Chief Inspector three years later. He was the Boss Man of the Ashington Force and he had a good team working with him: Inspector Alan Sanderson, CID Sergeant Jim Kellman, Detective Constable Ned Givens, Sergeant Mather, Sergeant Charlie Wilson, a nice fellow, Sergeant Billy Ball and Detective Constable Hector Clark. All grand lads who respected the Boss greatly. Another Sergeant I musn't forget: Frank Douglas, Jim's right hand man, P.C. Fred Walker, a canny lad, and Gordon McLanachan, a tough Scotsman who went down to Newbiggin as Sergeant to take over the station there. And dozens of lads who passed through Jim's hands at Ashington who are now Inspectors and Chiefs themselves all over the country.

Jim and Barbara MacKintosh had three children: Ann, Barbara and John. Both girls married policemen while John is serving in the Edinburgh Force as a piper in *The Edinburgh Police Pipe Band.*

Jim paid regular social calls to the *Portland*. He liked a drop of whisky and enjoyed hearing a yarn or two. He often had a drink with Weldon Laing and Hylton, his son, who were local butchers. They were usually with George Brown, an old drinking pal. They enjoyed a pint or two of *McEwans Special*. Weldon and Hylton were both directors of Gateshead Football Club at that time and were well known in the Football Association.

One night while we were having a drink, Jim told me he had been invited with a friend to a day out at Kelso Races by the Ashington *Constitutional Club*. It was their annual outing and everything was paid for. It wouldn't cost me a penny and would I like to go? "The trip is on Saturday and we'll have you back for opening time, 6 pm." It was like a command from God! It was an offer I couldn't refuse. I said "Yes, by all means."

He said, "Right, well, that's fixed; we'll pick you up outside the *Portland* at 9 am on Saturday morning."

Saturday morning came. It was a lovely November day. The sun was shining and not a breath of wind. Ideal for racing over the jumps.

We arrived at Kelso early enough to have a walk around the course, after a long bus ride. The jumps looked formidable, made with telegraph poles and brush wood on top; a frightening sight. We came off the course and into the refreshment tent for something to eat before racing started.

After our meal we made our way up to the Parade Ring for the first race. Here we bumped into Major William Norman Sample, dressed in his jockey colours, coming out of the changing tent. I knew Major Sample quite well. He was the Land Agent for the Duke of Portland Estates and he visited the *Portland Hotel* every six months to collect the Land Rents for the Duke.

I said "Hello, Major, are you going to win today?"

He recognised me and said "Try me each way." His horse was called *Brown Nugget* and it looked fit, so Jim and I had a flutter: a few bob each way. *Brown Nugget* won at 4 to 1 which made a grand start to the day. We backed two more winners that day and came away well into pocket. A wonderful day out.

Major Sample then lived in Bothal Castle and I asked him the next time he and Mr Batey came to collect the Ground Rents if he had any fear of taking those very formidable jumps.

He said "A large whisky just before the race helps."

In May 1956 I had a visit from a tall, dark bearded lad called Peter Deuchar, grandson of the Newcastle Brewer. He told me he had been running a *New Orleans Jazz Club* in Melbourne Street, Newcastle for a year and he had a number of requests from Ashington members to start a Club in Ashington. The *Portland* had been recommended and would I be interested in helping him to start a Club in Ashington?

I said "It sounds interesting. What about a few more details."

He told me there were six in the band and they called themselves *The Vieux Carre Jazzmen and Skiffle Group*. They were all keen to play in Ashington, and, if I was willing to let them use the music room to form the Club, they would arrange to start as soon as possible. I asked how much would it cost me? Peter said that the membership should take care of the cost, but, in the meantime, if I would be willing to help out with the cost of the transport – say about three pounds per session, that would be a great help until they were established.

I said, "Fair enough, when can you start?"

He said "Would Tuesday nights suit you?"

I said, "Excellent, it's a quiet night usually; that would be fine."

"OK, we'll make it Tuesday, 5th June, and see how it goes. That'll give us time to let our members know and time for you to advertise the opening of the Club."

New Orleans Jazz came to Ashington on June 5th, 1956. The instrumentalists were 22-year-old Peter Deuchar, banjo and skiffle group vocalist; Peter Gascoigne, 21, trumpet; Ronnie Robinson, 23, clarinet; Peter Coles, 19, trombone; Ged Ward, 31, bass; and Jim Stewart, 24, drums. A well disciplined group, all wearing red shirts and black jeans, devoted to jazz, and eager to please the audience. Trad jazz went down well with numbers like *Just a Little While to Stay*, *Shut Eye* and *The How Long Blues* which set the feet tapping.

The opening night was a success; both band and myself were satisfied with the outcome and jazz became a regular weekly feature at the *Portland Hotel*. Peter Deuchar and I got on well together; we understood each other. He looked after the band and I looked after the pub. We became good friends. This was also the year that the Royal Air Force Association organised a *Carnival Week* in Ashington to bring back the old community spirit that Ashington had enjoyed before the War. Bob Johnson was Chairman of the Committee in charge of the project and he called into the *Portland* to ask if I'd be willing to help. They had planned a full programme, starting with a waiters' race on the Monday night and would I be willing to enter? Another offer I couldn't refuse. I said "Yes," I would enter and help him in any way I could for the benefit of the community. He told me that Tommy Dobson, the Manager of the *Grand Hotel*, had entered his head barman, Jimmy Dixon, to race on his behalf, and a number of workingmen's clubs had entered their waiters to run in the race. Monday, 2nd July, was race night. It was a beautiful summer's evening, warm and balmy. Fourteen waiters and one waitress lined up in the race which was started by the Chairman of the Council, Mr Colin McNiven. I was standing next to the Councillor and Jimmy Dixon was next but one away from me. Mr McNiven had some trouble with the starting pistol. It misfired then fired in quick succession. This gave both Jimmy and myself a flying start on the rest of the field. Jimmy was four or five yards in front of me at the top of the Station Bank and all the way up the main street towards the *Grand*. I thought I'd do a Chris Chataway on him and catch him on the tape, but opposite *Woolworths* I over-ran myself and fell to my knees. Jimmy Dixon won the Pewter Pot by a distance while two waiters from the *RAOB Club*, Bill Patterson and Marshal Ferguson, were second and third. I took a lot of stick from the customers about falling in the race, such as, "Fancy letting little Jimmy Dixon beat you!" "You're hopeless!" But it was all good fun and the thousands of people watching the race seemed to enjoy it. I got more publicity from falling in the race than I would have done if I'd won it.

On the Wednesday afternoon I received a frantic phone call from Alex Cummings, manager of the *Harmonic Hall*, asking me to come and help him with the Baby Show he had offered to run for *Carnival Week*. He had expected a dozen babies to turn up for the Show which was to be judged by the local District Nurse. When I arrived at the *Harmonic*, Alex and the Nurse were surrounded by two or three *hundred* irate mothers and crying babies. It was pandemonium and choking hot in the hall. I helped Alex to get them all seated, but it was hopeless. They just kept coming. It was decided by the Nurse to march them all around to the People's Park; line them up and judge them there. By this time, the mothers were near to riot. I decided to disappear and leave Alex 'Holding the Baby' so to speak. I couldn't handle all those mothers; it was a nightmare.

The level-headed District Nurse gave each baby a number and

drew the winning number out of the hat. It was the only possible answer. *Every* mother had the best baby in Ashington. What was she to do?

When they heard about the Baby Show, the Carnival Committee were worried in case it brought them any adverse publicity; they wanted it hushed up. Undaunted, Alex rang me and asked if I could borrow an old pram from anyone. I told him Mrs Brown, who lived above Richardson's shop had a pram she used to take the washing in to the laundry. "I'll ask her if we can borrow that."

She agreed to lend us the pram when I explained what we were going to do and said "You can have the pram; anything that'll cheer us up. Why not?"

The Carnival Committee had a Comic Football Match arranged with the Round Tablers that night; a 7 pm kick-off and Alex's idea was to get dressed up as a baby: nappies, bonnet and all; get into the pram and I was to push him all the way down the main street to the *Grand Hotel*; turn left down to Portland Park Football ground. Then parade around the pitch with Alex holding a placard with "Wot, no Baby Show?" written on it. We raised a few eyebrows on the way down the street. When we got to the *Grand Corner*, we saw Sergeant Mather on point duty controlling and directing the crowd down Lintonville Terrace to the Football Ground. Alex was in the pram and I was dressed in long linings, a bright red jersey and a bowler hat with the top cut out. We went up to the Sergeant and asked the way to the Football Ground. He took it good humouredly and smiled, stopped the traffic, and directed us down towards the ground in a most theatrical manner, which gave the crowd a good laugh. Alex was lying in the pram drinking a bottle of *McEwans Pale Ale* through a rubber tit, enjoying himself immensely. We did two circuits of the pitch with the pram, joined in the match for about fifteen minutes, then Alex, feeling he had made his point, whatever it was, said "I've had enough, Bill, how about you?"

I was completely exhausted and said "Let's get back to the *Portland*."

On the Friday night before the Big Carnival Parade I was approached by one of the Committee, a lad called Jimmy Middlemass, who asked if I would be willing to ride on a float with a young beautiful blonde girl, portraying a business man with his secretary sitting on his knee with the caption

'AUTOMATION WILL NEVER REPLACE THIS'

Of course I said Yes. It was like a bonus for the work I'd put in for the Carnival. Jimmy said "Can you be at the Hirst Welfare just before 2 pm for the start of the Parade?"

I said "OK, but why don't you bring her in tomorrow lunchtime and introduce her before the Carnival and explain what we have to do?"

Jimmy said "Right, I'll do that."

Saturday morning was a busy time at the *Portland* normally, and the morning of the Carnival was no exception. The *New Orleans Jazzmen* turned up to play in the Parade, and I arranged it with Harold Anderson to supply one of his fruit wagons to use as a float for the Jazzmen. About 1 pm in walked Jimmy Middlemass with an attractive young blonde. She looked like a film star, with a fur cape slung across her shoulders, high heeled shoes, mini skirt, mini tube suntop and a bunny-girl collar and mini bow tie, and as brown as a berry – what a stunning girl! The pit lads were all eyes, and asking "Who's that, Kell?"

I said "I think we're in the carnival together. I'll let you know later."

They all said "You lucky sod."

We were formally introduced and she knew the part she had to play in the Carnival. I had very little to do but sit at the desk and look like a business man. The situation we portrayed spoke for itself and, in the Parade, she got all the wolf whistles and I took all the banter and funny remarks. We did win a prize in the Parade, but what it was or what it was for, I forget.

The Carnival Week was a huge success. The weather had been perfect and all the events had been well supported by the people of Ashington. A week to remember.

Not all the Show organisers were as lucky in 1956. It was a terrible year for the annual Ashington Flower Show. The headlines in the *Evening Chronicle* read "N.E. Show 'Gates' Hit by Weather: Heavy Cash Loss" and in the *Ashington Post* on 22nd August, 1956, the headlines read "Treasurer tells public meeting £400 needed to save The Flower Show. Appeal to be made to social clubs and trades people."

The Flower Show was held in the Peoples' Park and I myself had witnessed the complete wash-out and devastation the weather had caused the Show. All that hard work and care in growing the blooms and other exhibits, a complete wash-out because of the atrocious weather. It was their 70th Flower Show and it looked like being their last. I approached some of the customers in the *Portland* with the idea of starting a 'Save the Flower Show Fund' and, if they agreed, I would be willing to donate £10 to start it off. The Show needed £200 to pay off their debts and £200 to start next year's Show. The customers committed themselves to try and raise at least £200 to help the Ashington Flower Show survive. With a little publicity and support from the *Ashington Post* and the *Ashington Advertiser*, it began to take off. At a public meeting in the *Excelsior Social Club*, Mr Syd Turbill, the treasurer of the Ashington, Hirst and Bothal Horticultural Society, thanked myself and the customers of the *Portland* for our effort to save the Show and the president, Mr Alan Robson, added that Mr Curtis Absalom, proprietor of the *Harmonic Hall*, had offered the prize money in the Baking Classes of the industrial section. With the help of trades people, the social clubs, the Ashington Mineworkers' Federation and the Ashington Football Club, the Flower Show was saved for at least another year.

The President of the Horticultural Society, Alan Robson, was our local press reporter. He represented the *Newcastle Evening Chronicle*, *The Journal* and also covered for the national press, anything of importance that happened in the Ashington area. A quiet, unassuming, thoughtful man, who did a lot to project Ashington in a favourable light. He tried desperately to make reportable sense of some of the statements that a lot of dafties in Ashington used to make. A kind man and a good reporter.

The following year the Carnival was repeated as before and I was asked to run again in the waiters' race. Alex Cummings and I agreed to run and we both decided to make it a fun run with no intention of trying to win. Councillor Jack Mather was Chairman of the Council and he took on the duty to start the race. There were eight men and one woman running that year. Mary Robson was representing the *Grand Hotel*, and little Billy Barnes was running for *The Portland*. They were both placed but one of the lads from a Club won it.

The Flower Show also went ahead that year and, as a reward for my efforts to save the Show, I was given the licence to run the Beer Tent. The Flower Show Committee had insured against being washed out by rain and would be reimbursed if that happened. Unfortunately that August Saturday we had gale force winds of up to 80 miles per hour and, at lunch time, Chief Inspector MacKintosh came into the Beer Tent and informed me that he had decided to clear all the tents because of the storm danger. The Beer Tent started to rip and, by 2 pm, it was in shreds. The rest of the Show tents were ripped and torn to pieces by the terrific gusts. That day marked the end of the Ashington, Hirst and Bothal Horticultural Show. A complete disaster.

1958 was the year of the *Hula Hoop*. The headlines in the *Evening Chronicle* on Wednesday, 29th October, read "Pit Town Mad About Hula Hoop" and in the *Newcastle Journal* on the 3rd November it read "Hulla Hoop Craze Hits Ashington." Harry and Rowley Gray, who ran *Hall & Cardwells* Music Shop, reported extraordinary sales. They couldn't get enough hoops to keep up with the demand. Such was the craze, I decided to start a competition to find the 'Hula Hoop Champion of Ashington.' With the help of the band and Billy Todd we organised heats of three at a time, the winner going into the next round and so on until we got three finalists. It was a winner! The music room was packed every night we had the competition on. We arranged the Final for a Sunday night. There was hardly room for the Finalists to swing their hoops, but we managed to get it under way. The Hula Hoop Champion of Ashington was a 33-year-old; Iris Little, from Bamburgh Terrace. And, with my encouragement, she issued a challenge to all-comers 18 and over, for the North East Championship title to be held the following Sunday night at the *Portland Hotel*, Ashington. Second was Mrs May Brown a 38-year-old mother of six of Ingleby Terrace, Lynemouth, and a close third was Billy Oliver, a motor mechanic with a handle-bar moustache, of North Seaton Road, who was also our accordion player. Even the Captain of a tanker 'had a whirl'. He was Captain Alan Patton of Institute Road, Ashington who was married to Sally Phillips and was flying to Bahrain the following day to join his ship *The Coltex Karachi*. The Hula Hoop certainly brought a lot of business to the *Portland*, the time the craze lasted.

That same year Limbo Dancing was becoming popular on television, done expertly by coloured Caribbean dancers who made it look so easy. I decided to try it out at the *Portland*. Rusty's brother, Wilf, made the Limbo stands and the pole to dance under and, with the co-operation of the band and concert chairman Billy Todd, we announced another competition: a limbo Dancing Competition. The miners were used to working in low seams down the pit in a crouched position, but trying to dance under a low pole, bent over backwards, wasn't their forté. After two weekends of the competition, we ground to a halt. They were all off work with 'bad backs'. It was just too much for them.

Another character who used to call and see us when she was visiting her sister in Ashington was Nancy Geldert, a dynamic, flamboyant workaholic, who ran a small pub in the Lake District in a place called High Lorton, near Cockermouth. This five-foot dynamo, with the aid of her husband, Jack Geldert, ran a small country pub called *The Horse Shoe Inn.* Jack also worked full time as a salesman with Rickerby's of Carlisle and was a character in his own right; a marvellous combination to run a small country pub. Nancy was the mirror image of the actress Thora Hird and the character who Thora often plays on television. Nancy always spoke with an exaggerated posh accent whenever she was introduced to anyone she thought was of any importance, until she got to know them and then she would revert to her normal broad Geordie dialect. Always a twinkle in her eye, and great fun to be with. *The Horse Shoe Inn*, Lorton, was renowned for its food and hospitality and could accommodate six to ten residents.

The first time Rusty and I decided to visit her, I rang Nancy to ask if it was convenient. Nancy answered the phone in her very posh voice: "This is the Horse Shoe Inn, High Lorton."

I replied "Hello Nancy, it's Bill Kell. Can Rusty and I come to stay for a few days?"

Nancy said "Oh, it's yee. Aye, cum any time ye like. You're welcome whenever ye cum."

The *Horse Shoe* was a rustic little pub with a small bar, ten customers and it was crowded! Only enough room behind the bar for Jack to serve the clients, with one large, long room which acted as lounge and restaurant-cum-concert room. It had an upright piano standing at one end which was played by the local joiner, a dark-haired lad called Tommy: a real pub piano player. Nancy had a large repertoire of songs and jokes and could keep the party going at anytime; she liked a bit of fun, and we had some grand nights. Marlene, Nancy's niece, helped her run the pub, a dark-haired, pretty girl, always had a friendly smile and very eager to please. She looked after the residents and was a great asset to Nancy. It was like 'home from home' at the *Horse Shoe*. Jack and Nancy had been running *The Bridge End House* in Lorton as a boarding house when the tenancy of the *Horse Shoe* became vacant, and, as Jack was one of its best customers, he applied for and got the tenancy from Jennings Breweries of Cockermouth.

For our few days' stay, Rusty and I made the *Horse Shoe* our base to visit as many Lakes as possible in the time we had. The weather was fine and warm; ideal for travelling in the open MG. We would spend the whole day away and get back in time for dinner in the evening. Each day we took a different route. From Lorton to Cockermouth then on to Workington, Whitehaven, Cleator Moor, then down to Ravenglass across to Coniston Water, Grasmere, Keswick and back to Lorton. Another day we went via Loweswater, Buttermere, up over Honiston Pass around by Derwent Water into Keswick for lunch then on down to Ambleside, Troutbeck, Windermere, Bowness then back up over Kirkstone Pass, Borrowdale, Keswick and back by Bassenthwaite Lake and home to the *Horse Shoe*.

We visited Wordsworth's Cottage in Grasmere, like stepping back into history. We also had a trip over to Appleby, where the travellers were gathering for their Annual Fair.

The day before we left, Rusty and I went into Cockermouth to buy Nancy a present for her kindness to us on our stay. At the end of the Main Street in Cockermouth there was an antique shop owned by a woman in her early sixties. You could tell she had been a bit of a girl in her day. Most businesslike. We bought a set of framed hunting prints for Nancy which we thought she'd like. While we were in the shop I saw an old Army bugle and asked how much the old girl wanted for it.

She said "Four pounds ten shillings."

I said "OK, I'll take it," and bought it to bring home to the *Portland*.

Nancy was pleased with the hunting prints and told us that the Melbreck pack of hounds met every Boxing Day at the *Horse Shoe* and that Billy Irvine, the nationally known huntsmen, and Major Iredale, the Master of the Hunt, were great friends of hers.

The night before we left, Jack called me to one side and said "Bill, you're an expert on beer. I've got a problem with mine. It always seems to happen on a busy night. As soon as we start getting

Back to the Portland, 1955

busy the beer goes as flat as a fart! I can't understand it. Can you tell me what's wrong? The beer is always alright through the week, on quiet nights. It only seems to happen when we get busy."

I said "OK, let's have a look behind the Bar." His pumps were OK, his drainer was clean and the glasses on the drainer were OK. He had the proper glass rinse supplied by the trade to clean the glasses. I said "Everything seems to be fine here. Explain to me what happens on a busy night."

Jack shouted for Nancy to come and listen to what was being said. He said "When I start to get busy, Marlene comes behind the bar to help and Nancy comes from the kitchen to wait on and collect all the empties."

Nancy said "That's right. I collect all the empty glasses and bring them to the bar. If the bar is crowded I take the odd tray of glasses to the kitchen and wash them in there."

I said "What do you wash them with?"

"Just warm water and a drop of washing up liquid."

I said "Washing up liquid is the worst thing you can use on beer glasses. It knocks the head clean off the beer."

Nancy and Jack just looked at each other without saying a word. I said "Now we've found the problem, we can solve it. If you have to wash the glasses in the kitchen, put a handful of salt in the warm water, then rinse them in clean, cold water. The salt acts as an antiseptic and kills all grease marks on the beer glasses and, if you do the same in your drainer bowl behind the bar, Jack, that should solve your problem."

Poor Nancy, she didn't realise what she was doing wrong; she had the look of a whipped dog and went off into the kitchen for a quiet weep.

The following morning after a marvellous breakfast we got ready to leave. Nancy, Jack and Marlene came out to the front of the pub to wave us goodbye. Jack shook my hand and thanked me and said, "I'll see you when we come through to Ashington, Bill. Pleasant trip." Nancy had got over her upset and was her usual cheerful self, as bright as a button, in her clean, white nylon overall. She wished us a safe journey and off we went back to Ashington and home. Jack and Nancy were to become a great influence in our business lives in the years ahead.

Rusty's sister, Lily and her husband Bob, had been running the *Portland* while we were away. She had also been looking after Leonie and everything had run smoothly. Leonie was fine, and pleased to see us back home. It had been a pleasant break. One of those short holidays that you look back on with fond memories.

Back to work, the lads in the bar appreciated the bugle I had brought back from Cockermouth and had a lot of fun with it. Little Geordie Armstrong was the best of a number of buglers amongst the lads. He had learned to play while he was in the RAF Cadets, Ashington Branch, (ATC). Geordie got the job of announcing with a bugle call, anything of real importance that happened in the Bar. The winner of a raffle; the finalists of the Sunday morning domino handicap which Jimmy Rodgers usually organised. The bugle was used for any announcement that was made when the Bar was packed full. One busy Friday night we had a call from the local Round Tablers. They were dressed as cowboys and indians. While they were standing at the Back Bar enjoying a drink, little Geordie blew a call on the bugle and Johnnie Rodgers screamed out "Indians!" The whole Bar burst out laughing.

From 1958 on, a lot of changes were taking place in the trade. Small independent breweries were being taken over by larger companies and the trade was much more competitive; especially in Ashington. Most of the Working Men's Clubs were extended with a lot of money being spent on alterations and redecorations, converting the old shop front image into something more like the image of a pub-cum-club. Further up the coast at Seahouses a fellow called Jack Britton who had the *Links Hotel* had opened up another place called *The Seafield Restaurant* to run dinner dances with a late licence. Bus loads of my customers were going up to Seahouses every weekend. To rub salt into the wound, the buses used to pick up these passengers outside the *Portland* every Friday and Saturday night. I asked a passenger one night what was the attraction at Seahouses? He said, "Well, Bill, you can have dinner when you get there and after dinner there's dancing, and you can drink until 12 midnight and you're back home by 2 am."

I thought, well, what's to stop me doing that? I've got the room upstairs. It just needs a little organising and a lot of hard work and we could offer the same facilities. All I had to do was convince the

Back to the Portland, 1955

Breweries it was a worthwhile idea. That wasn't easy. With a big Brewery company there's always some creep in the office who is jealous of your success or who just doesn't like you. That can put the block on anything you're trying to get done. The favourite comment was, "Well, there's been a change of policy and we have decided to leave it for the moment." Very frustrating. Whenever this happened Rusty and I would just change tack and approach it from another angle with the same goal in view. It usually worked.

Meanwhile, there were a few changes taking place at the *Portland*. Polly Buglass had taken over the Buffet from Peggy Wilson; Belle Reay and Olive Hamill had been joined in the Bar by Doreen Ross, Carol Sweet and Edie. Three new barmaids. The band had a few changes too. The piano player was replaced by Sid Jackson and Bobby Jackson, his brother, became the new acting, unpaid Concert Chairman. Bobby Jackson had a nice way with him. Great personality and popular with the customers. He could sing and could be very persuasive. He could convince anyone that they could sing, so we were never short of vocalists in the Concert Room. Sid and Bobby seemed to inject a new enthusiasm into the band. They took on a new lease of life which was infectious and the customers liked it. One Friday night Bobby Jackson approached me with an idea of starting a *Spot That Tune* game which had been made popular on TV by a beautiful blonde singer called Marian Ryan. I said I thought it was a good idea, but how much would it cost me?

Bobby said "Very little. If you put in a pound, the band will add a pound each night. It will soon mount up and will be a prize worth winning."

It was a huge success. The idea was that anyone who sang a song would have their names put into the hat and if drawn out they had the chance to *Spot That Tune*. Sid and Bobby were choosey about who they allowed to win. It was always a regular customer, well known to the band, who won. Albie Burton and Billy Neary were regular winners. I don't know how they did it. I wasn't worried; as long as it filled the Concert Room I was quite happy. After all, it only cost me one pound per night to generate a lot of business.

Ashington's Swinging Sixties

In the early Sixties a revolution took place in the pub entertainment business. Out went the piano and drums and in came the twanging guitars. Young groups were the 'in thing'. Pop groups had arrived. To keep up with the modern image, the band had two young lads join them, both guitar players. Harry Smith on electric guitar and a big thick-set lad whose nickname was 'Hoss', on bass guitar. A new sound and a new lease of life for the band, right up until *Discotheque* came on the scene.

Early in '62 I was approached by a group of youngsters who were interested in running a fortnightly dance at the *Portland*. They said Wednesday or Thursday night would be suitable if I'd be willing to let them have the use of the Concert Room. They wanted to form their own club with suitable members and it would be run on proper lines.

I said "That sounds fine, Wednesday is free, you could give it a try to see how it goes."

Within two weeks they had formed a committee comprising two lads and three lasses. James Wright, a 23-year-old schoolteacher; Bruce Bishop, a 20-year-old dental student; Angela Cairns, treasurer, 20-year-old civil servant; her sister Diane, an 18-year-old shop assistant; and Janice Parker, an 18-year-old typist. They had their own ideas about decorating the room on dance nights. Large pictures of pop stars and pop groups, low lights etc. They asked my permission to put candles in wine bottles on each table to give the room an exotic atmosphere, after which they named it *The Candlelight Club*.

I soon realised that there was a whole new section of business to be developed by catering for the younger customer. *The Candlelight Club* grew in membership and I gave them every encouragement to develop it. Within a short while, the fortnightly dance became a *weekly* feature. This was just the leverage I needed to convince the Breweries that they should go ahead and open the upstairs rooms for dances and catering functions. After a long chat one day with

Jack Ross, my outside manager at that time, Jack said "I know the Breweries don't want to spend any money at the moment, but if you are willing to go ahead and do it yourself, I'll give you a note to go through to the Breweries' warehouse and pick what second-hand furniture and fittings you'll need to open it up yourself."

Rusty and I were thrilled. That note and permission were all we needed. A canny fellow, Jack Ross. He had given us a free hand to develop the first floor of the *Portland* to our advantage and the Brewery's, of course. The catering and any other functions would be ours as long as we sold the Brewery's products. Within a week I had been through to the Brewery stores to see what was on offer. I got a furniture van full of assorted pieces and other items that would be of use. The lads in the stores were helpful. They gave me the best of what was going. Over a hundred bentwood chairs, two dozen assorted tables, one dozen trestle tables, one well-used back bar fitting, two high gantries to hold the barrels, two upholstered bench seats. They didn't have a bar counter but said they would get one for me as soon as possible. Everything had been discarded from other pubs and hotels the Breweries had, but you can't look a gift horse in the mouth. We were pleased to have them. It was a start. The beginning of what became a distinctly profitable business.

On the first day of May 1961 the first betting shops were opened in Britain. This made quite a difference to our morning trade in the bar. The three bookies' runners we had at the *Portland* were all paid off, and the backstreet bookies all became legitimate, opening betting shops up on every street corner. Charlie Chisholm, an established bookie in Ashington, opened a shop in the Middle Market and another one in High Market, just up from the *Portland*. Davey Grant opened up a shop just two doors away from us on Station Road. Before those shops opened, all those punters would have had to call into the *Portland* or one of the Clubs, to put on a bet. By one Government Act, we had our morning trade cut to shreds and no one could say or do anything about it, because the previous method of placing their bets was totally illegal in pubs. I remember the tale about Ozzie Redshaw, the local poof, who had just collected his money on a winning bet when one word came over the tannoy: "objection." Ozzie was on his way out of the shop when little Davey Grant shouted to him "Objection Ozzie," and Ozzie replied in his queer voice, "I'm not bloody objecting, pet!" and bounced out of the shop.

In a month or two, the morning trade settled down. After all, the pit lads still liked a pint and a crack with their pals. We still had the nightshift lads calling in for a drink before they went home to bed, but it was never quite the same after the betting shops opened. I was discussing this one night with Chief Inspector MacKintosh and he told me that within a year or two all the small betting shops will be either closed or gobbled up by the big boys and less than a dozen bookies will be running the betting across the whole country. His prediction was totally correct or as near as makes no difference. Jim MacKintosh liked a joke and he thoroughly enjoyed telling a joke. He told me about the little Tyneside comedian, who was booked into a big Catholic Club in Newcastle where two weeks previously, the Steward had ran away with the week's takings. As he walked onto the stage he noticed a life-sized crucifix hanging at the back of the stage. He went up to the microphone and, nodding to the crucifix, he said "I see you've catched the Steward!"

Mac was a loyal friend, with a clan-like loyalty that I have found a lot of Scotsmen have to one another. If you were a friend of Jim's you were a friend for life and, if he could do you a good turn he would. A canny *Poliss*.

It was Christmas Eve in the early sixties. I had to drive up to Lloyds Bank on Station Road to get extra change for the holidays. The Saturday street was busy and I had difficulty in parking the car. The bank closed at 12 noon in those days and I had only a few minutes to spare. I managed to squeeze in between two cars parked outside Crisp's Toy Shop, opposite the bank. I'll admit the back end of the car was sticking out onto the road a bit, but I was in a hurry. The bank was full and I had a long wait in the queue. When I got home with the change I noticed a small white slip of paper stuck under the wiper. It was a notice to produce my licence at the Police Station within 48 hours, signed PC Kerr. I had been pinched.

I phoned the Station to find out what it was all about. Sergeant Charlie Wilson answered the phone. I asked to speak to Jim MacKintosh. Charlie said "He isn't here at the moment, Bill, I'll put you through to his home number." Jim answered the phone and I told him "I've just been pinched by one of your lads for parking. I've got a ticket that says I have to take my licence to the Station."

Jim said "OK Bill, just do as they say and they'll sort it out."

Off I went down to the Station, parked outside the front entrance and, as I got out of the car, I saw PC Kerr coming out of the door, adjusting his helmet.

I told him "I've brought my licence. What do I do about this ticket?" He seemed to be agitated and in a hurry to get back on duty. "Just forget about it, Bill. Tear it up and throw it away and, er, Bill, don't mention this to MacKintosh, will you?" Case closed.

There was an unwritten rule at Ashington Police Station in Jim MacKintosh's time, that no drunks were to be arrested on New Year's Eve. They were to be treated in a friendly manner and sent home, if at all possible. As Michael Caine says "Not a lot of people know that!"

I remember the tale about the Ashington councillor – no names, no pack drill – who called into the Station one New Year's Eve to give the Sergeant and the lads a drink from his bottle. After a while he fell into a drunken sleep in the back office. When the relief Sergeant came on duty, he had the councillor carried through and put to bed in one of the cells. When he woke the next morning, there was hell on. He was most indignant about being treated like a common criminal and locked up in a police cell. The road to hell is paved with good intentions. Profuse apologies were made at all levels and the episode was hushed up at the request of all concerned.

In the *Ashington and District Advertiser* on the 29th July, 1960, the headlines read "Screaming Women and Strewn Seating in Hotel Riot." What had happened was on the Saturday night, 9th July, we were visited by two busloads of trippers from Blakelaw, Newcastle. They had come through for a night's drinking and entertainment at the *Portland*. We ushered them into the Concert Room where Bobby Jackson and the band made them very welcome. In the summertime we catered for bus loads of folk from Newcastle and the surrounding district every weekend with little trouble. In the course of the evening, Joe Locke, the barman-waiter, told me "There's one or two Worky-Tickets amongst this lot Boss."

I said "If they give you any trouble, tell them to behave themselves."

The tension began building up and by 9.30 pm it exploded into an almighty battle. Little Joe came running in behind the bar holding his face. Somebody had given him a black eye. There were between 20 and 30 men fighting, hitting each other with stools and tables; there were glasses flying in all directions. Some of them were local hard lads who had just joined in for a little excitement. We couldn't manage to control two bus loads of strangers, so I called the police. It took over a dozen bobbies plus an Inspector to sort them all out. Some went to Ashington Hospital and some were taken to the Police Station before being sent home. Only four were charged with being drunk and disorderly, but we were left to clean up the mess. We had six bins full of broken glasses; stools and tables to clean up; and a lot of blood to wash from the walls and floor.

At Ashington Magistrates Court on Thursday, 28th July, the presiding Magistrate, Mr T. Patterson, fined the four defendants £2 each saying "You cannot go into places like this and break things up. There is nothing to smile about," he warned them. "We are giving you 14 days to pay, but if you come back here, you will not get that chance."

Inspector J. D. Hogg told the Magistrates there were two bus loads of people and it was quite impossible to deal with all of them. One of them, a hod carrier called Dodds, said "There were more than us involved." Then asked for time to pay. The cheeky swine! The local lads who were involved in the battle were easily picked out by their bandaged heads, stitched chins and black eyes. I didn't say anything to them about the fight. I overlooked their involvement, especially when the main instigators were fined only £2 each. Normally, they would have been barred for fighting. From that night, I made up my mind I would build up my own security force within the staff to cope with any trouble that might come our way. All the part-time and weekend barmen had to be strong and fit and at least 12 stones in weight before I'd employ them. The bigger the better!

In a large pub you have to be prepared for all sorts of things happening. One busy Friday night, I was standing in my usual place at the top end of the bar talking to Alex Watson and Alex Logan when a customer came up to me and asked me if I could settle an argument he was having with his pal who was standing at the other end of the bar.

He said, "Can you tell me how many pints there are in a quart? I say two and my pal says four."

I told him he was right: there were *two* pints in a quart. He went back up the bar and ordered two pints of beer from Winnie, the barmaid, and when she asked for the money he said "Oh, Kell's paying for these," and shouted down the bar to me "Isn't that right, Kell? Two pints?" I put up two fingers and shouted back "That's right, two pints." The barmaid shrugged her shoulders and carried on serving.

The merger of the two big breweries in the North East came about in 1960. *Newcastle Breweries* and *McEwan Younger* of Edinburgh became Scottish and Newcastle Breweries. What had been our most bitter business rival had now become our partner. The only three pubs in Ashington now belonged to the same company. We were all under the same management: *Newcastle Breweries*, run from their head office in Newcastle's Haymarket. This meant a whole new set of bosses because the *Portland* had been a *McEwans* pub since 1937. The merger went a lot smoother than I thought. There were no drastic changes. We still sold the same beers, *McEwans*, with a little extra choice such as *Newcastle Brown Ale*, *Amber Ale* or *IPA* if you or your customers preferred. No pressure to sell any one kind of beer was put upon the managers. The patriarchal head of Newcastle Breweries at that time was Colonel Porter, Managing Director, one of the old school of brewery bosses. He was accorded the utmost reverence by the team of directors and management staff under him. A proper old gentleman, who knew the brewery business from A to Z. His son, Henry, was also a director, with Kenneth Saxby, Licensed Houses Director in charge of over 1000 pubs and hotels. David Stephenson was Brewery Secretary; Norman Thompson, Head of Staff; and Jack Barras, Area Outside Manager. A good team. They all did their jobs well.

After things settled down, it became the company's policy to show their new managers around the brewery. We were selected a bus load at a time to be taken through to Newcastle Breweries in the Haymarket, and shown every aspect of the brewing of their beers from the malthouse to the finished product. Colonel Porter took it upon himself to show us around the Bottling Plant of which he was understandably proud. There were thousands of bottles of beer going through the plant that day being filled and sealed with a crown cork. The finished article was examined by two girls looking through two large magnifying glasses at each filled bottle as it passed on the conveyors. Porter took us up to a large glass-fronted office to see the whole aspect of the plant from an advantageous position. As we watched, we all noticed the two girls were talking away to each other, paying no attention to the bottles as they passed the examination glass. Colonel Porter remarked "There you are, ladies and gentlemen, one of our greatest problems. The human element. That's how you, very occasionally, get a foreign body into your bottle of beer. Now that's what we're up against."

Over 60 years ago Colonal James Porter, who was then head brewer, began developing a new product called *Newcastle Brown Ale*. He spent three years in the company of Brewery Chief Chemist, Mr Archie Jones, perfecting the ale, which over the years, has become nationally and internationally known as *Newcastle Broon*. The product came on the market on 25th April 1927, and was advertised in the local press as *Entirely New, You've Tasted Nothing the Same as This Before!* It became the North East Working Man's Champagne. It certainly gives you a lift, but you need to give it the utmost respect – it can get hold of you. It has been given some peculiar names in its time: *Fantastic*; *Brown Dog*; and *Lunatic's Broth*. Whatever they call it, it is still a popular drink and will still be going in another sixty years. I can still picture Colonel Porter as he was then: smart, military bearing, military moustache, hair parted from the left and brushed down flat to his head, hooded eyelids, kind face. A perfect Northumbrian gentleman. There's not many like him around now.

The last time we saw him, he presented Rusty and me with second prize in the Best-Kept-House Competition. I quote from the *Evening Chronicle* on 4th November 1963,

---

'WELL-KEPT HOUSE'

The Portland Hotel, Ashington has won second prize in a Best-Kept-House competition organised by a brewery firm. The 70 year old hotel is managed by Mr & Mrs Bill Kell. The hotel, which has recently undergone extensive alterations, was beaten into second place by a new building. Mr & Mrs Kell will be attending a special luncheon in Newcastle to receive a cheque and congratulations for their success.

We received a cheque for £25. That's the hardest £25 we have ever worked for. We were on for weeks cleaning the place from top to bottom; everything was sparkling and shining like new. Kenneth Saxby and Jack Barras inspected our work and honoured us with second prize. We and the staff were quite proud of our achievement, after all, there were a lot of pubs in the competition and we were prizewinners. Rusty gave the cheque to the staff to split up among them: they had worked hard for it. The only disappointment we all felt was the size of the cheque – a miserly amount.

The Newcastle Breweries was started by a Gateshead lad, John Barras and Company, which was founded in 1770. It was later bought by the North Eastern Railway Company. With the cash he acquired, John bought the Tyne Brewery and, in 1890, several small breweries in North Shields, Gateshead and Sunderland, linked with him to form The Newcastle Breweries Ltd and that's how it all began. Following the First World War, the *Blue Star* was adopted as the company's trade mark and in the 1950s, Robert Deuchar Ltd, of Newcastle and Duddingston, James Deuchar of Newcastle and Montrose and John Rowell & Son Ltd, of Gateshead, became part of The Newcastle Breweries.

The *Portland Hotel* soon became the centre of social activities for the younger set. We had *New Orleans Jazz* in the Music Room; a juke box in the Starter's Room; a Honky Tonk piano in the Back Bar; and we had Rock Groups in the Candlelight Rooms upstairs. The place was really jumping. A swinging place to be if you were young enough to enjoy it. The young lasses promenaded from upstairs down through the Back Bar to the Music Room at the end of the passage in their skin-tight, ultra-short mini skirts. Then back along the passage, through the Back Bar and up the stairs in a leisurely fashion to show the lads standing at the Back Bar what beautiful legs they had.

It was the first meeting place for many a married couple. They all met at dances at the *Portland Hotel*, Ashington in the Sixties. The opening of the upstairs rooms proved a huge success which helped the breweries to decide to spend some money on developing the project. They put in a new bar at the head of the stairs; a dance floor in the large dining room; and refurbished the rest of the rooms which made it look like a night club and a separate unit from the rest of the pub. Now we were ready to start catering for private functions. Rusty had passed her course in catering with credits in 1953 which was run by Bill Forsyth, the Secretary of the North East Licensed Trade Defence Association. She was presented with her catering diploma by Colonel Nicholson, Managing Director of

Vaux Breweries of Sunderland at that time. This was now Rusty's chance to show what she could do in the catering field.

My wife has never been afraid of work and she had plenty to do to organise the equipment needed to cater for 120 people and staff to serve them. Nancy Geldert offered to come and help in the kitchen until Rusty had settled into the routine of the job. Nancy's experience in the catering trade gave Rusty the confidence she needed for those first few weeks of her catering career.

Rusty took Nancy through to the *Blackbird Inn* at Ponteland to buy a lot of catering equipment from the tenant who was retiring. She also had help with catering equipment from Mr Lupa of *Isons* the wholesalers of Stowell Street, Newcastle. He put himself out to get the right stuff at the right price for us and it was much appreciated.

Rusty's next job was to organise the kitchen staff and waitresses. In the kitchen she had, including herself, her sister Lily, Nancy Robinson, Elsie Jacques and Nancy Geldert. The waitresses came as a team. They had all worked for David Absolom before his tragic early death. They were Olive Metcalf, Mary Randall, Nellie Riddle, Lucie Ledger, Etty Cowell, Olga Green, Gertie Mitcheson and David Ireland. Behind the bar upstairs, we had young Donald Warrender, Les Imrie and Ella Robinson. After the meals were served and cleared away, David Ireland and Ian Spencer worked as wine waiters. On the whole, an impressive team.

While all this was going on, one of the dregs of society – a proper pain in the neck – stole our bugle.

We received plenty of publicity about the bugle; it was in all the local papers, but we never recovered it.

The year of 1963 proved to be a momentous one for Rusty and me. We opened up the dining room with our first big function on 15th February, 1963. The occasion was the annual dinner for the Ashington Branch of NACODS. When I applied for the extension of licence at Ashington Court for this function, I was asked by one of the magistrates "What's NACODS?" I told him it was The National Association of Colliery Overmen, Deputies and Shotfirers. What a mouthful. After a titter ran round the court, I was granted the licence.

Norman Davison, the owner of the *Ashington Advertiser*, sent his photographer to take a snap of the principals of the function and get the story for his paper. John Laws took the photos and the story was in the paper the following week.

The article under the photograph read:

> Twenty-five years ago, a publican arrived in Ashington with the intention of opening the long-dormant upstairs dining room in an Ashington hotel. But the war intervened and it is only now that his son has been able to get the job done. On Friday evening, the new dining rooms at the Portland Hotel, Ashington were opened, newly decorated and restored to their former likeness as one of the town's premier social spots. The occasion was the annual dinner of the Ashington Branch of the National Association of Colliery Overmen, Deputies and Shotfirers, which was attended by 120 guests.
>
> In the picture, the Association's branch secretary, Mr George Garbut, greets guest of honour, Mr Jimmy Dobson, new manager of Newbiggin Colliery. President, Jack Hamilton is on the left, treasurer, Mr T W Jackson, centre and, looking on, is Portland Hotel host, Mr Wm Kell. Mr Kell's father was manager at the Portland Hotel for many years.
>
> Mr Kell told the *Advertiser* that the cutlery used on the opening night, silver with the hotel name engraved on it, was some of the original bought by his father 25 years ago for the same purpose. It had been wrapped and put away and was as good as new.

I could always depend on Norman Davison to give me a good write-up and to publicise the pub and the business whenever he could. He and Charlie Marshall, his brother in law, who helped run the printing business were a great help to me whenever I needed any local publicity. John (Jack) Laws of Woodhorn Studios was also most obliging whenever I needed his help.

The heading in the *Daily Mirror* that day read: *Keep Calm*. Rusty cut it out and stuck it on the kitchen wall. It proved a great help that night – catering is a nerve-wracking job. However, everything went well and George Garbutt came through to the kitchen after the meal to thank Rusty and the staff. The menu that night was written out by Rusty herself as follows:

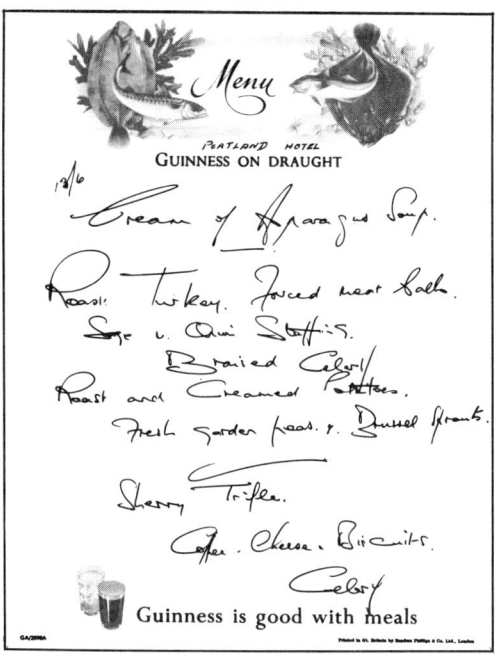

Rusty did that meal for ten shillings and six pence per head and still made a small profit. I don't know how she did it. The Brewery were happy because they had the extra business from 120 punters, drinking all night until midnight. That was the beginning of a long and eventful catering career for Rusty and I.

In 1962, we heard that George Dand had a young Shetland Pony for sale. George had a small farm up at Radcliffe crossroads, so we went up to see the pony. When we saw him, we decided right away to buy him. He had a long black mane and tail, four black legs, and a dark brown coat. Exactly what Leonie wanted. We paid £40 and George Dand delivered him to the Portland Stables. He was partly broken and Jack Amos, a retired storekeeper at the pit and an old horsey man, volunteered to finish his schooling with the help of a fourteen-year-old girl called Elsie Dixon, who was mad about horses. The pony's name was *Sooty*: a quiet, lovable little thing. He stole all our hearts.

Early in '63, Leonie decided to move up to the New Moor School of Riding for some extra schooling for *Sooty* and herself. The principal of the school was Thomas Dodds, an ex-African professional jockey, and his assistant instructress was Miss Carol

Skinner. It was a well-run little school: the first in Ashington. Thomas Dodds had one of those faces that had been lived in a long time; a leathery, weather-beaten skin, hooky nose and a twinkle in his blue eyes with a well-rehearsed smile that had been used regularly on all those racehorse-owning toffs who he had met throughout his racing career.

One cold Saturday morning early in '63, I drove Leonie up to New Moor for one of her riding lessons. *Sooty* was resident at the school and had become a firm favourite with the rest of the riding pupils. That morning I met an attractive, well-spoken lady who had brought her child to the school ror a riding lesson. She was the wife of a doctor in Blyth. When she heard I was in the hotel trade, she told me there was a nice hotel for sale in Seahouses, if I was interested. It belonged to a Mr Robinson: *The Wyvis Hotel* with ten bedrooms, overlooking the harbour. I said I was certainly interested and would go up to Seahouses with Rusty and have a look at it. The following Monday I phoned Mr Robinson for an appointment to view the hotel. He confirmed it was for sale and added "I want £10,000 for it not £9,999 – no offers. £10,000 is the price."

I said I understood and I would ring him back. In 1963, £10,000 was a large fortune, especially to a pub manager in Ashington. How would I go about getting ten grand? I first tried my bank, *Lloyds* in Ashington. The Manager told me they did not lend money on hotels and obviously wasn't interested in my application for a loan.

I mentioned this to Jack Geldert who had just retired from the licensed trade and was living in Ashington. After leaving the *Horse Shoe Inn* at Lorton, he'd had the tenancy of the *Curwen Arms* at Workington and then moved to *The Pier Hotel* at Hern Bay in Kent, which he had just sold. He was interested in the *Wyvis Hotel* and said he would be willing to go in with me in the purchase of the place. I told him I would have difficulty in raising the money. He said "Leave that to me. I'll take you to see *my* bank manager at Barclays in Ashington and we'll sort things out."

The bank manager's name was Mr Dawson, who came from Seahouses and knew the *Wyvis* very well. Mr Dawson's family had been fishermen at Seahouses for generations so he knew what we were talking about. He was interested in my ideas for the redevelopment of the hotel and said if we put in £2,500 each, he would lend us the other £5,000 to buy the place. Jack said we would do that and the loan was agreed.

Jack, Nancy, Rusty and I drove up to Seahouses, and over coffee in the *Wyvis*, we sealed the deal with Mr and Mrs Robinson and bought the place.

The *Wyvis* was a non-licensed residential hotel. Our idea was to turn it into a fully-licensed hotel and yachting club. Both the *Wyvis* and Seahouses itself were crying our for development in '63.

Arrangements were made for Jack and Nancy to move in and take over the running of the hotel to get it ready for our first season. Rusty and I carried on as usual at the *Portland* and, whenever we had the time, we visited Seahouses to see how Jack and Nancy were getting on, and to discuss the running and development of the place.

The *Wyvis* was built like a castle, overlooking the harbour. It had cement-rendered castellated walls with French windows looking in onto a beautifully lawned inner garden in the centre of the building. We decided it needed a face lift before the season started so we asked Rusty's brother, Billy Mann, a painter and decorator, if he'd go up to Seahouses and paint the whole place, inside and out. He agreed to do it at cost price and took his two lads, John Wyness and Brian Robson up with him. They made a grand job of it and it looked like a new building when they were finished. They painted the outside walls with a cream-coloured cement paint and the building shone out like a Spanish Castle on a hill.

Jack and Nancy quickly settled in and soon had the place running smoothly with the help of two young girls, one from Seahouses and a blond girl from Shilbottle. Early in the season, Jack had a visit from a couple of gentlemen, a Mr Leech and a Mr Bell, both local builders. They told him they were interested in buying the *Wyvis*. They also said they knew what we had paid for it and they were willing to offer £12,000. Jack told them he had a partner in the venture and didn't think he would accept £12,000. Mr Leech said "If your partner doesn't accept the offer, you know what he can do with his hotel."

Jack said "Thank you. I'll let you know what he has to say." After they left. Jack phoned that night to tell me what had happened.

I said "Why didn't you take the offer? £2,000 is a tremendous profit."

Jack said "They're both millionaires. I think they'll pay a bit more. We'll leave them to think about it. They obviously want it for some reason."

Jack didn't hear from them again until one Sunday in July '63, the day of the Queen Mother's visit to Seahouses and the Farne Islands. When the Royal visit was over, Leech and Bell turned up at the *Wyvis* with a better offer; £12,500. Jack accepted on condition they would let him fulfil the bookings he had until the end of September, and he would then hand over the first week in October. It was agreed – to my great relief. We found out they wanted the hotel for a Holiday Home for the underprivileged old people of the North East. So that was the end of the *Wyvis* as a non-licensed residential hotel.

After all the loose ends were tied up, Jack and I came out with a clear profit of about £2,000 each. It was an experience for me, and taught me a lot. I had a number of sleepless nights over it and the worry of how I was going to pay off the debt to the bank. Fortunately, it worked out well in the end. Jack and I were two happy men.

1963 was also the year I met a De Lane Lea dancer called *The Bongo Baby*. I used to watch her at least twenty times a day doing her dance number. A beautiful coloured girl. I felt I knew her well. But I'll let a cutting from the *Sunday Sun* of 24th November, 1963, tell the story. The headline read:

SHE'S HIS ANSWER TO RIVALS AT ASHINGTON

Outnumbered by a score of competing social clubs, an Ashington publican has charged into the all-out battle for business with a secret weapon – a juke box showing sound films. Surrounded by expensively renovated luxury social clubs, bearded Mr Bill Kell of the Portland Hotel has added to his normal entertainment service for customers a cinebox. It serves up snappy song and dance motion pictures in colour at a shilling a time.

Top of the bill is selection No. 29, a rip-roaring, drummed-up dance routine by a curvaceous, dusky charmer dressed in a minimum of red feathers and No. 29 is Mr Kell's answer to big prize bingo sessions, variety shows and dance nights at the elegant social clubs in his neighbourhood.

A score of his customers, with drinks in their hands, stood with backs to the bar watching the juke box film last night. Mr Kell said "Since I installed this gadget, I have been selling six barrels of beer more in the bar a week. That is 216 gallons or about 1700 pints. News of the juke box is getting around. The other night a party of men

> made the journey from a town eight miles away to see it and satisfy their curiosity about No. 29." A man in the bar interrupted his close scrutiny of the dancing girl to say "I was up in Alnwick this week and met a man who knew all about No. 29."
>
> Looking at the performance of the *Bongo Baby* which he has now seen hundreds of times, Mr Kell said "I call her the ultimate deterrent to bingo."

The agent who had the machines came from Whitley Bay, a canny fellow, in his fifties, who told me that the machines weren't paying their way – too costly to maintain. They were eventually sold and were all shipped off to Australia.

1963 was the year that Ronnie Harrison came to Ashington to take over the *Harmonic Hall*. We became good friends. He was the only customer who ever came to offer help when I was having difficulty with an awkward punter. One Friday night, while I was escorting this gent out of the *Portland* for misbehaving, giving me a lot of trouble, kicking and scratching, Ronnie came up to me and said "Do you want a hand, Bill?"

I nodded and he grabbed hold of the lad and, between us, we put him out without any problem.

Ronnie spent a great deal on rebuilding and refurbishing the *Harmonic Hall* whose postal address was 111 Station Road, Ashington. On re-opening the place after the alterations he called it *The Three Ones Club* and it became the 'in' place to go after the pubs closed at night: a very popular venue.

Ronnie was a Hebburn lad and served his time with *Reyrolles*. He was also a professional football player who signed for Wolverhampton in 1940 and later went to Gateshead for five years. He broke his leg while playing at Gateshead, then went to Darlington. In '47 he came to Ashington and finished his career in football with the Colliers, playing with such players as Sammy Scott, Gordon Dent and a Widdrington lad called Proudlock. In 1958, Ronnie started promoting dances in halls all over the North East and, on 8th January, 1960, he left *Reyrolles* and took up dance promoting as a full-time job. He never looked back. It was dance promotion that brought him to Ashington and the *Three Ones*. Ronnie was a man of hidden depths, a man of influence. Over the years, I learned a lot from Ronnie Harrison.

Another man that I met in '63 who was to have quite an influence on me was David Moody. Davey was a haulage contractor, a self-made man. When the war ended, he came out of the RAF and went to work as a bread van salesman with Guide Post Co-op. After twelve months, he decided to go to work for himself and bought a registered coal business with one wagon from an old man called Mr Snaith of Netherton, near Bedlington. With hard work and a tenacious business sense, he soon had a fleet of wagons. In the early days, Davey could work twenty hours a day non-stop for weeks, when he was in the process of building up his business; a real tough guy. He had recently bought George Beatty's coal business in Institute Road just behind the *Portland* and with it had inherited old Geordie Nichol and his horse and cart. That was also part of the coal business. Davey used to bring old Geordie into the *Portland* for a drink occasionally and that's how I met him. Geordie Nichol was one of my regulars. He had also been one of my dad's best customers. I had known Geordie since my boyhood; a canny fellow, always a smile, always full of fun, a nice, nice man.

Another fellow I knew in the early sixties who could truly claim "I did it my way" was a dapper little man called Jack Richardson known locally as *Bingo Jack*. A hard working, hard living Showman who had his regular gaff down behind Woodhorn Road; a bingo stall that he ran every night entertaining the locals with his humour and showman's patter. He gave value for money. His prizes, he claimed, were always the biggest. I asked him one night if he could get me a multi-coloured blanket that I wanted as part of my costume for a Fancy Dress Ball which Rusty and I were going to that Friday night at the *Harmonic*. Rusty was going as a Red Indian maiden and I was a Mexican Bandit with the blanket tied over my shoulder. Jack said "Leave it to me. I'll get you one for Friday."

Sure enough, on the Friday morning, he walked into the Back Bar in his overalls – his working clothes – with the coloured blanket folded over his arm. He said to Big Olive, the barmaid, "Is the Boss in?"

Olive said "He's upstairs – but he doesn't want to buy any blankets today – so on your way."

I'll leave it to your imagination as to what Jack said in response to that. He came charging up the main staircase shouting, "Are you there, Kell?" I met him at the top of the stairs. "Who is that cow you've got down there? She told me to get out, I only came in to give you the blanket." After profuse apologies, Jack calmed down and said "Well, anyway, I hope you both have a good night at the dance."

Jack was a shrewd, very clever little man. To have travelled showgrounds up and down the country all those years and still have all your own teeth was visible proof.

One Saturday afternoon we were busy preparing for a dinner and dance for 120 guests. It was our first function booked by the Ashington Police Force, when up the stairs came Jack Richardson carrying a large cardboard box. He said "You've got a do on for the local bobbies tonight?"

I said "Yes."

"Can you place these on the table for each guest?"

I looked in the box and there were 60 boxes of chocolates and 60 packets of five cigars.

Jack said "Don't say who's brought them."

A very shrewd gentleman.

Arthur Silver was another astute man who I became acquainted with in the early Sixties. Arthur and his wife, Peggy came to Ashington on 11th November, 1957, to take on the management of the *North Seaton Hotel*. They took over the pub from Mr and Mrs Jimmy Watson. It had been a Robert Deuchar's Hotel which had been taken over by Newcastle Breweries. Before coming to Ashington, Arthur had managed the *Newburn Hotel* at Newburn-on-Tyne, and had also spent a few years managing *The Portland Hotel* in New Bridge Street, Newcastle, opposite the *Oxford Galleries*.

Arthur was interested in the politics of the trade and soon became deeply involved in the local LVA which was The Blyth and Morpeth Licenced Victuallers' Association. After joining the committee, he soon became Treasurer and along with Stan Gray, Chairman, and Bill Straker, Secretary, helped to revitalise the LVA. Bill Straker had the *Hastings Arms* at Delaval. All three of them worked hard to make Blyth and Morpeth LVA a successful association.

It is Arthur Silver I have to thank for getting me involved with the LVA. He kept at me to go to the meetings – to become involved – to become interested. He eventually succeeded.

It became a way of life for Arthur Silver. In the 60s and 70s, Arthur was known throughout England and Wales for his work with the Licenced Victuallers. He was Chairman of Blyth and

Morpeth LVA; North-East President in 1969; he became Vice-President of NALHM – 'National Association of Licenced House Managers' in 1969 and became President in 1970. He helped to form NALHM and put a lot of work in for pub managers all over England and Wales. He liked doing it. He enjoyed helping managers who had got into difficulties. Arthur and I were deeply involved in Licenced Trade matters right up until he sold the lease of his pub on 1st August, 1980.

Meanwhile, back at the *Portland* in 1964, Rusty and I found it difficult to get time off from the business. We were so busy.

One night early in 1964, January or February, it was a Tuesday, our day off, and it got to 8.30 in the evening before we both could get away for a break. We had to be back for just after 10 pm so were limited in our choice of places to go. I suggested we had a run out to Widdrington, twenty minutes' drive from Ashington, to visit a quaint old pub I knew called *The Junction Inn*, known locally as *The Bus*. Rusty agreed. Anywhere for a change.

The *Junction* had been a Beer Shop with a six-day licence for over a hundred years, and, in 1947, the tenant applied for a full, seven day licence which gave him permission to sell beer and spirits seven days of the week.

The night we called they had no spirits for sale. Nothing to offer, only bottled *Amber Ale* which they had borrowed from the *Widdrington Inn* to accommodate a few locals. The pub was dying. It was right on the bottom. The girl behind the bar served us with a bottle of beer and said she was sorry she had nothing else to offer. There were about ten locals in playing darts. Curly Tennent was sitting on a chair near the fireplace. Nellie Tait was playing darts with Wessel Sedonic, Bill Murryfield and Ginger Ken Cowan.

The pub was basic: a lead-covered counter with three beer pumps with lead pipes running under the floor to an old lean-to cellar at the back of the bar. Flagstones on the floor; a kitchen table in the middle of the bar floor with three or four wooden bench seats. It had one side room in much the same condition; the bar and the room had the original oak beams.

When we came out, I said to Rusty, "What do you think of it?" After a long pause she said "It could be quite nice."

I said "It's up for sale you know,"

"Why don't you buy it?"

I didn't answer.

The following day my father rang me from the *Keel Hotel*, Dunston, asking me to look for a house in Ashington for him. He told me that some young hooligan had butted him in the face and broken his jaw and he wanted to be out of the trade. He'd had enough; he was 64 years old. The locals had arrested the thug and kept hold of him until the police arrived. He was fined £100 for assaulting my father.

Rusty and I discussed the situation and, later that day, I phoned my father with a proposal. I told him there was a small country pub for sale at Widdrington and, if I bought it, would he be interested in looking after it until I was ready to take over.

He said "It's not *The Bus* is it?"

I said "Yes."

"OK, you're on."

The Kells Up The Junction

In 1964 the *Junction Inn* was owned by Hammond's Breweries. I contacted Louis Johnson, the estate agent, to approach them with an offer to buy the pub on my behalf. After a day or two, Louis got back to tell me Hammond's had received a tentative offer of £2,800 but they were haggling and if I offered another £100 it would be mine. I told him to go ahead and offer £2,900. Hammond's accepted the offer and *The Bus* was mine.

George Bilton, the Newbiggin solicitor, acted on my behalf and completed all the deeds and legal details that were necessary. Father took over the *Junction Inn* on the first Monday in March, 1964. There was no need to negotiate any loans. I paid cash for it with the money I had made from the sale of the *Wyvis Hotel*, so I had no financial worries on that score. It was a long-term investment as far as I was concerned.

My father was his own boss. He ran the pub his own way. No outside managers from the Breweries to worry about; no stock-takers on his back. His main job was to build up the business in his own way, without any hassle from anyone. Dad was one of the best publicans of his time in the North-East – he knew the job. Any major decisions which had to be made with regard to the pub, he always referred to me. "You'll have to see our Bill," was his cry.

Jack Sanderson, the Wine and Spirit Merchant from Morpeth, told me this when he called to see me at the *Portland*. He said, "I've been to call on your father at the *Junction* to see if he would open an account with us for wines and spirits, soft drinks etc. He told me it was *your* pub and I would have to see you. As you know Bill, we have supplied the Kells here at the *Portland* for many years. We're old business friends. And now that you have branched out on your own we would like to supply you at the *Junction* with whatever you need. I know it will have cost you to buy the *Junction* but if you are finding it difficult, financially, I'd be willing to give you six months' credit until you can get on your feet with the business."

I have never fogotten that kind offer from Jack Sanderson – a real gentleman and exceptionally kind man. He got the account. Fortunately, I didn't have to take him up on his offer. But I gave him my business right up until his death many years later.

My parents, with the help of my sister Dora, ran the *Junction*. It was an instant success. The pub had a new lease of life and, with dad being known so well in the area, he had a steady stream of customers from his days at the *Portland*. All his old pals called to see him. When you went into my dad's pub you not only got a drink, you were entertained with the banter from behind the bar or between my father and the other customers who were already in the bar. Always a warm friendly atmosphere whenever you called.

My main job at the *Junction* was to refurbish and update the facilities that were necessary, as tastefully as possible, to bring the pub into the 20th century. With the help of Rusty's brother, Wilf the joiner and Mavin Storey, the builder, from Newbiggin, and his young assistant, Bill Kilburn, we started to knock doors out of windows. I told the customers we paid for the alterations with the lead we stripped off the counter.

Alan Thirwell was an electrician with some innovative ideas about lighting up the pub. John Moore worked with Alan, and they made a great job of it. We also called on the services of an expert bar fitter to finish off with a back bar fitting; a new copper top on the original counter; copper-topped tables with real oak chairs to go with them; leather covered bench seating around the walls of the bar and the room; lino on the bar floor; and carpet in the room. That was it. We were ready for business.

We had pulled out the old brass beer pumps with white porcelain handles (which I later donated to the Beamish Museum) and installed a new Keg beer that Scottish & Newcastle Breweries were introducing onto the market at that time. The new beer was called *Starbright* which was served through a cooler up to an attractive blue-coloured font on the bar. It was perfect for the situation we had at the *Junction Inn*. There was no cellar work, as such. When one keg was empty, another was wheeled in from the old lean-to cellar and clamped on to the beer line. The ale was cool and always in perfact condition, ideal for the job.

With the first phase of the alterations completed, I left my dad to get on with the running of the pub. I called every Monday morning to collect the takings and see if anything was needed for the smooth running of the pub. Then back to the *Portland*. That was the routine for the first year.

Meanwhile, back at the *Portland*, I had taken Ronnie Harrison's advice and began running the dances myself with the help of young Peter Curran, Maureen Staines and Mary Ramsey. I booked the groups myself. The most popular at that time were *Rue and the Rockets* from Carlisle; *The Don Juans*; *The Rebels* from Rothbury; *The Black Hawks* from Blyth; *The Trek* and *The Wild Ones* from Chevington. I had a list of around 100 rock groups to choose from in my file and, if anyone let me down at the last minute, I could always count on Ivan Birchall's Agency to send a group he had on standby for such an emergency. Birchall never let me down. He always answered the phone himself in those days whatever time of day or night it was – always keen for business. On the rare occasions when we just couldn't get a group to turn up we gave the dancers a rain-check for the following dance night. We never refunded the money – always gave them a rain-check.

Late in '63, Rusty and I decided to try and liven up Monday nights at the *Portland*. Monday night was quiet, so we thought we would try running a supper dance and cabaret night once a month on Monday nights. It was quite a project and took a lot of organising. I approached Benny Kirtley, a local lad and one of the best piano players in the North-East. He was delighted with the idea. His trio had played for me on a number of occasions at our dinner dances. He had Percy Jobson from Morpeth on bass and Walton Owen, also from Morpeth, on drums. They made a smooth sound; easy to dance to.

I also approached Lillian Russell and asked her if she could get together a resident troupe of dancers for our chorus line. She was tickled pink with the idea and said she already had a troupe who had been dancing at *The Blue Parrot Club* in Dunston: Margaret Sweet, Sylvia Clements, Moira Black and Jean Lambert. They called themselves *The Showgirls* and decided to rehearse with Benny on Sunday mornings to get the show together. All we needed now was a star for the show and our first star was Mercury recording artist, Ethna Campbell, who had appeared on Tyne Tees Television's *One O'Clock Show*. A beautiful, dark-haired Irish girl with a lovely personality. The show was a sell-out; one hundred and twenty tickets at ten shillings each. A huge success. Everyone enjoyed it and wanted to know when we were having our next event. Our cabaret nights became a regular feature. We even got a mention in *The Stage and Television Today* magazine, written by Alan H. Brown. I quote from 13th February, 1964:

> Ashington, for those who don't know, is a mining town in the heart of Northumberland. The last place in which one would expect to find a night club! Yet there is one, in the rambling *Portland Hotel*, enthusiastically run by mine host, bearded Bill Kell.
>
> He and his wife, Rusty, converted the upstairs lounge into "The Cabaret Room", installed proper lighting and sound equipment, and began by opening it to the public on a ticket only basis, one night a month. Result: booming business. Cabaret acts who have appeared there include recording artist, Ethna Campbell, Tyne Tees Television's Larry Mason and Spanish singing discovery, Chus Cuesta (who incidentally, was recently congratulated by Frank Sinatra Jnr after his one-night stand at Al Burnett's Stork Club in London). The Portland cabaret also has something that many other night clubs lack: a resident troupe of dancers called "The Showgirls".

Alan Brown was a free-lance journalist interested in the theatre, television and any showbiz artist of interest. Always on the lookout for new young talent, he managed one or two who starred in our cabaret. Linda Kaye was one of his artists who worked for us. A young, pretty blonde girl, with a lovely voice and always a success in our shows. The King Sisters were another act he managed who worked for us; two bonny girls, just starting out in show business with pleasing voices.

Alan Brown was also kind enough to publicise our little show at every opportunity. He wrote in *The Stage and Television Today* magazine on 12th March 1964:

> The big city may look down its nose at the small town: but when it comes to cabaret, there are one or two things to be learned from Ashington, Northumberland.
>
> I went to the Portland Hotel to catch spanish tenor, Chus Cuesta, topping the bill in cabaret there – and as usual, the audience just wouldn't let him go. If anyone in the Rose Counties is interested, he's due to appear at the Ace of Clubs, Leeds in April.
>
> On the bill with him were the Kevin Hedley trio – a local talented singing group who play accordion, bass and guitar – and improve with every performance. The surprise attraction of the show, however, was the Can-Can, danced with considerable verve by The Showgirls – under ultra-violet lighting recently installed by manager, Bill Kell. The effect was luminous, colourful and startling.

> Magnificent support was given to the acts, as always, by the Benny Kirtley trio, Benny himself used to play regularly at the Blue Parrot, near Newcastle. Nor was the inner man forgotten. Bill Kell's charming wife, Rusty – having prepared a six-course dinner for the hundred-and-odd guests and then gone on to serve in the bar – still found time to make me a bowl of steaming-hot Romany soup. Altogether a splendid evening!

It was nice to read and also pleasing to know that your efforts are appreciated.

Someone in New York must have also read the article, because on 10th April 1964, I received a letter with the heading:

Birney Golden – Circle Artists
1674 Broadway Suite 610
New York 19, New York   Plaza 7-4668

Cabaret Room
Portland Hotel
Ashington, Northumberland
England

Gentlemen

The Golden Gate Quartet, currently on a six month tour in Japan, will be available 15th July out of Paris. They are scheduled to open in Monte Carlo 21st August for two weeks and at this writing, available immediately after.

May I have the pleasure of a reply advising your interest.

With many thanks and kindest regards.

Sincerely yours

Birney Golden

Sitting reading that letter after breakfast that morning, I smiled quietly to myself and handed the letter to Rusty. After reading it she said, with a twinkle in her eye: "That's Show Business, Bill!"

Poor Birney. I didn't reply to his letter – little did he know that after selling all the cabaret tickets, I had only £60 to put on the whole show, including the supper! Still, we had some great nights. Memorable evenings.

Eric Nichol starred in one of our shows. He rehearsed with Benny and the Showgirls for a month to put on a *Black and White Minstrel* type show. He did a medley of Al Jolson songs with the girls joining in. They did, *Dixie, April Showers, Mammy,* and *Carolina in the Morning.* They had everyone singing. An audience likes nothing better than a good sing song. The show was an outstanding success. Eric Nichol had star quality. A great entertainer, good comedian, an all round showman, who worked hard at his trade – entertaining.

The cabarets were such a success that we began offering a cabaret spot with our dinner dance bookings at a little extra charge to cover the cost of the artistes. They were successful and soon became a regular feature in our programmes.

One of the regular stars in our cabaret shows was a girl from Tyneside called Kay Wight; a beautiful, dark-haired, dark-eyed girl, who could put over a ballad professionally; a girl who made the audience love her. A lovely personality, always turned out immaculately and did her job well. A real professional. When she starred in the show you could guarantee a great night. The format to our success was planning. We covered every possible eventuality, but life is full of surprises and there were a number of occasions when things just didn't go according to plan.

One night after I'd ushered the main guests upstairs and left them at the bar for drinks before dinner, little Etty Cowell, one of the waitresses, came downstairs to tell me that the guests were about to go into dinner and all the electricity had gone off in the kitchen. Now, anyone who has catered for over 100 guests will know the feeling of panic that can come over you when that sort of thing happens. I ran to the fuse cupboard at the top of the bar, checked the fuse marked 'kitchen'. It was a 30 amp fuse and it had blown. Below the kitchen fuse was another fuse marked 'stables and outhouses'. I took it out. It was OK, so I pushed it into the fuse marked 'kitchen' and the power was restored upstairs. The feeling of relief was terrific – excellent.

On another occasion, we had a special evening for the local Constabulary, a dinner dance and cabaret with the Principal Guest of Honour – Chief Constable Cooksley and his wife and friends. The reception went beautifully and dinner was going well until we got to the sweet: sherry trifle. I had Victor Vizeur and Davy Ireland waiting on the top table – two very good, top-class waiters. As Davy was swinging his tray full of sherry trifles piled high with fresh cream, one tipped over and gently squelched down the back of Chief Constable Cooksley's dinner jacket. Davy panicked and ran into the kitchen crying his heart out. Victor ushered the Chief Constable through into the kitchen where Rusty sponged and cleaned his jacket. Davy sat in the corner of the kitchen sobbing like a child.

I asked the Chief if he would have a word with Davy to try and calm him down. The Chief went over and said "Don't worry, son, it could happen to anyone." Dave profusely apoligised and the Chief said "That's OK son, – but could you point out the Constable who paid you to do it?"

Deputy Chief Constable Bob Scott and his wife and friends were the guests at another function the local police were having. Bob Scott was a big bull-necked man, a typical old-fashioned bobby. Monsieur Hercules Poirot he was not. Though he had the happy knack of catching and convicting most of the villains in his divisions, which was proof enough of his ability.

After dinner that night, while the staff were clearing the floor for the dancing and cabaret, Chief Inspector Ken White came up to me and said "Can you do me a favour Bill? Will you have a drink and a chat with the Deputy Chief? I can't keep up with him."

Big Bob Scott liked drinking large *Johnnie Walker* Black Label whisky, and as soon as I spoke to him he said "Will you have a drink, Mr Kell?" and promptly ordered two large ones. One for him and one for me. You *never* refuse a drink from a Deputy Chief Constable. After a few drinks with him I was asked to do the introduction to the cabaret.

Chus Cuesta the Spanish tenor was the star of the evening. He had trained at the Dusselldorf Conservatoire, and sung at the Milan Opera House. I made a note of this with the intention of using it in my introduction.

In front of the mike, and after a number of large whiskys, I couldn't get my tongue around *Dusselldorf Conservatoire*. After three goes at it, Walton Owen, the drummer, said in a loud stage whisper "Sit doon, Kell, you've had too much." I sat down and when the introductory music ended I stood up and announced in a loud voice "Ladies and Gentlemen, Chus Cuesta," and walked off, passing Chus on his way on, with an astonished look on his face. Being the professional he was, he carried the show off without a hitch.

I spent the rest of the night in the twilight zone. Rusty came to my assistance at the end of the evening, checked the tills and made sure everything was locked up and then put me to bed. The end of a rough night.

It was during the Sixties that I became involved with Ashington Football Club. The team had been doing badly and were deeply in the red. They were *always* in the red. Anyway, Norman Stafford and Albert Anderson, who were the leading lights on the board then decided to bring in some local businessmen. So I was drafted in along with people like Eric Nichol who ran a coal business, Ronnie Harrison, then managing the *Three Ones* nightclub, Louis Johnson the estate agent, Eddie Clark of Ashington Engineers and a few others.

I knew absolutely nowt about football. But when the club refurbished their clubroom and got their liquor licence, I was able to lend a hand with that side of the business. First of all we had to go up to Bothal Castle, home of the Duke of Portland who had been the original owner of the land, hence the name *Portland Park*. It was there we saw Major Sample, the Duke's agent, and we were able to persuade him to give us the go-ahead to serve liquor.

We began to get a canny team together. Ken Prior who had played for Newcastle United came as player manager; before that we had Dave Davidson as manager, another ex-Newcastle man. We strung some good results together and the team progressed into the Northern Premier (then a feeder-league for the Football League). But that proved to be a big mistake. Away games to places like Macclesfield and Runcorn were so expensive to fund, especially if you had to stay overnight. So it wasn't all that long before we were back playing in the local league.

One highlight was the time we entertained a first-class Scottish team. Hylton Laing, through being on the FA committee, was quite pally with the Celtic manager, Jock Stein. Hylton persuaded Jock to bring his team down to play a friendly in a bid to boost our finances. And, apart from it being a wet night, it went well. Arthur Ellis, who took part in TV's *It's a Knockout*, was the referee. I forget the score, but the crowd of over 2,000 went away happy and we made a bob or two for the club.

The club just paid its way as and when it could. As far as I know we never went near the bank. We owned the ground so the bank knew its money was safe. But that is when we sold the ground to Ashington Council – I signed the deeds.

I handed over the reigns of chairman at the club to Bill Leslie who ran a business called *Vulcanisers* on the Jubilee Trading Estate. He had helped with the electrical side of the ground. We got some old searchlights from the colliery (they had been used to light the aerial ropeway which deposited the waste on the pit heaps) and with these old-fashioned big bulbs we were able to introduce floodlighting, of a sort. But it was mainly for training sessions on dark nights.

The directors were supposed to take turns to bring in a bottle of whisky so that the officials could have a little drink after each home game. They had a room in the club offices on the left just as you went in through the *Buff* turnstiles. But of course it always seemed to be muggins who was supplying the booze. And it all got to be a bit much, plus the fact that I had my own business to run, and the worry of the debts in the football club wasn't worth it. The bus company *Wansbeck Motors* were on to us for money – they hadn't been paid for months. One of the Grenfell family had the business then. He was very nice about the whole thing, but, I mean, howway, you cannot run business on sentiment.

When I decided to pack it in, I was interviewed by a BBC reporter who said: "Well, Mr Kell, and why are you leaving the club?"

"Business and ill health," I replied. "In fact we've done the ultimate: we've given the job to a Scotsman!"

The year of 1964 was a busy one for us. Going into business at the *Junction* on our own account was a massive step to take. George Bilton advised us to use *Greaves Grindle*, accountants, of Alnwick, and it was their firm's Arthur Bird who looked after our affairs.

Arthur was a sound, trustworthy man and a good friend.

One day in the early summer of '64 my dad phoned me from the *Junction Inn*. "Hey, Bill, there'a a fella here who's offerin' to instal a fruit machine in the bar."

This was usual after the 1963 Betting and Gaming Act had cleared the way. That was a signal for dozens of small businesses to begin supplying pubs all over the country with their own machines. It was a licence to print money for most of them.

Dad went on: "It seems a good deal cos it's not ganna cost us a penny. Aall ye have to dee is sign on a dotted line. Then this chap will apply to the Cooncil and to the local magistrate for an annual licence on wor behalf.

"OK, father, send him over and Aa'll sign."

The machine installed was one of the original one-armed bandits with the Red Indian head on the front and a pile of sixpences on show under a glass front, ready to drop for the winning punter. At a tanner a go it was phenomenally popular.

A couple of months later I rang dad: "Hoo much money are we rakin' in?"

"Oh, we're deein' canny, ye knaa, Bill, It's tekin a bob or two. But Aa just use it to buy some cheese and biscuits for the regulars on a Sunday mornin'."

I had to smile. "Fair enough," was my reply.

Last Orders, Please

One afternoon I called to see my father. There he was behind the bar with a few customers sitting on bench seats at the bar. One drunk who was standing at the counter began to call my father all the names he could lay his tongue to.

I stood and listened until I could take it no longer. "Father, just say the word and Aa'll hoy this cowboy strite through that door!"

A faint smile crept over dad's face, and he whispered: "Bill, bonnie lad, Aa was dealin' wiv this sort laang afore ye were born. Just leave him to me."

Within five minutes my father had so verbally castrated this chap he could have qualified for the top job in a sultan's harem.

It was yet one more lesson for me in the art of Keeping Bar.

In the old days back at the *Portland* on a Monday morning, the Sick, Lame and Lazy Club used to congregate just after opening time at 11 am. These were the lads who had been injured underground, others too frightened to go down the pit after a heavy weekend on the beer, and the rest who wouldn't have work in any shape or form.

One particular Monday they were all laying down the law because Sir Stafford Cripps' latest tax had hoyked up the price of beer and had put a tanner on a packet of twenty *Players*. But my father soon quietened them.

"Hey, does ye lot not knaa when yor weel off? Mark my words, afore varry laang you'll be payin' *ten* shillin's a pint for beor!"

"Impossible."

"Not in my lifetime, Aa won't."

"The government will nivvor gerraway wiv it."

These were some of the mocking replies.

"And Aa'll tell ye another thing," continued father. "Do ye see them pit-wheels up yonder?" pointing through the front window of the *Portland* at the Duke Pit winding gear. "When them wheels stop tornin', yous lot are finished ... and so is Ashin'ton."

He knew what he was on about, did my dad, owld Bill Kell.